Praise for Dementia, God & the Church

'Having known Wendy and Frances for several years, it has been a pleasure to read their excellent, well-researched book and available resources, explaining factors and pressures affecting dementia, and how faith can become more real and churches play an important role in this.'
Jennifer Bute, author of *Dementia from the Inside*

'Wonderful. May this book bless many people who are struggling to understand the sacred pilgrimage of dementia.'
Christine Bryden, author of *Dancing with Dementia* and *Will I Still Be Me?*

'*Dementia, God, and the Church* brings wisdom and insight to an area of church ministry that can be overlooked. It instils hope and urges courage in keeping people whose lives are affected by dementia at the heart of church and community. The book sings with compelling voices drawn from lived experience of dementia which gives it weight and authority in shaping responses to this growing area of need. Hope derives from the reality of God's Spirit continuing to work in lives touched by dementia, and the possibility we can make a difference even through small changes.'
Julia Burton-Jones, Anna Chaplaincy Training and Development Lead

'This hope-full book offers a stepping stone in exploring aspects of relational life for churches, with an invitation to cross the divide and break down the barriers of isolation so often experienced by people living with dementia and their families. Practical and inspiring examples encourage compassionate connection but, even more than this, to honour wisdom expressed by those living with dementia. They can be teachers of intimacy with God, who live in our midst yet find themselves on the margins. These are deep waters, but not too deep for God's love, which is seen and felt throughout.'
Debbie Ducille, Ministry Lead, Anna Chaplaincy for Older People

'This is the book I needed when I set out in ministry to older people, and has now provided me with wisdom and cause for reflection.'
Brian Dunlop, chair of Cheltenham and Bishop's Cleeve Anna Chaplaincy

'High praise for this compassionate and timely book, which offers hope and practical wisdom, and highlights the vital role churches can play in bringing God's love to people living with dementia and the families and friends who journey alongside them. As our population ages and more families are living with dementia, this book is an important and much-needed resource for the church and for us all.'
Alexandra Huggins, CEO, Faith in Later Life

'Faith truly is a mystery. This poignant book reminds and invites us to remember that God is thankfully not bound by our human cognitive capacity. It unpacks both theologically but also practically how we, the church, can play our role in supporting those living with dementia. It is written with tender, practical, authentic, sincere, love and care.'
Glyn Jones, church planter and lecturer in missiology, author of *The Peg and The Pumice Stone*

'This book engages with one of the big challenges of our time: how to care for and include those who struggle with dementia. It provides practical examples of how the needs of those living with dementia can and are being met, and advice about working with those who care for them as well as their families. Wendy and Frances record for us many examples of how these needs can be engaged with, and how a willingness to go on learning is the foundation for everything that is done in the name of Christ in this area of ministry. I hope and pray that many will read this book, and find the resources they need to go on caring courageously.'
Phil Dykes, Winchester Diocese

'*Dementia, God, and the Church* offers a compassionate and grounded account of dementia as a context in which personhood, dignity, and God's presence endure. Gleadle and Attwood skilfully weave lived experience with pastoral and theological insight, challenging assumptions that faith is primarily cognitive. This is an important resource for those in Christian ministry, equipping the church to respond with greater imagination, sensitivity, and hope to those living with dementia and those who care for them.'
Abigail Maguire, director of learning and student experience, Moorlands College

‘This book is backed with biblical references, careful argument, and vivid stories from those living with dementia, caregivers, and churches trying to serve both groups.’
Robin Thomson, author of *Living with Alzheimer’s: A love story* and *Unfailing Love: 30 devotions to encourage dementia caregivers*

‘Wendy and Frances’ inspirational book is of invaluable practical help as both fuel and a tool: fuel to remind us to cherish each person with dementia as whole people, loved by God and of infinite value; a tool to enable us to journey alongside others with everyday insights in sharing God’s love, reminding us that spirituality can blossom as cognition becomes limited. A word of warning, keep some tissues close as the stories within of carers and of those living with dementia are deeply moving.’
Chris Duffett, artist and creative evangelist, former co-principal of The Light College, and former president of the Baptist Union of Great Britain

‘*Dementia, God, and the Church* is a deeply moving and important book that speaks with wisdom, compassion, and hope into one of the pastoral challenges of our time. Wendy Gleadle and Frances Attwood offer a beautiful vision of dignity, belonging, and faithful community for those living with dementia and those who journey alongside them. Rich in theological insight and practical encouragement, this book calls the church to embody Christ’s love in tangible and transformative ways. It is an inspiring and grace-filled resource for churches, caregivers, and all who long for more compassionate communities.’
Miriam Baines, supporter engagement manager, Pilgrim’s Friend Society

‘I was so encouraged to read this book. Golden threads of faith, hope, and love are woven through every chapter. This is a deeply practical book, shaped by the wisdom and experience of people living with dementia and those who walk alongside them. Essential reading.’
Tina English, founder of Embracing Age and author of *A Great Place to Grow Old: Reimagining ministry amongst older people*

15 The Chambers, Vineyard
Abingdon OX14 3FE
+44(0)1865 319700 | brf.org.uk

Bible Reading Fellowship (BRF) is a charity (233280)
and company limited by guarantee (301324),
registered in England and Wales

EU Authorised Representative: Easy Access System Europe – Mustamäe tee 50,
10621 Tallinn, Estonia, **gpsr.requests@easproject.com**

ISBN 978 1 80039 433 9
First published 2026
10 9 8 7 6 5 4 3 2 1 0

Every effort has been made to trace and contact copyright owners for material used in this resource. We apologise for any inadvertent omissions or errors, and would ask those concerned to contact us so that full acknowledgement can be made in the future. See page 187 for full acknowledgements.

A catalogue record for this book is available from the British Library.

Printed and bound by CPI Group (UK) Ltd, CR0 4YY.

Wendy Gleadle
& Frances Attwood

Dementia, God & the Church

JOURNEYING WITH HOPE

From Wendy

To my children, grandchildren
and special friends (you know who you are) –
thank you all for your love and encouragement.
You're never too old for a dream to come true!

From Frances

To my husband, Phillip, for his support and encouragement,
to Sally Nevitt, for her inspiring ministry to seniors,
and to all families who struggle with dementia –
you are the real heroes.

Contents

Part II: How can churches better support families living with dementia?

Frances Attwood

Foreword

It is with great privilege that I introduce *Dementia, God, and the Church: Journeying with hope*, a profound and timely exploration of one of the most challenging realities of our time. In these pages, Wendy Gleadle and Frances Attwood guide us into the world of dementia with a deep sense of compassion and theological insight, offering not only understanding but also hope.

Dementia is a condition that evokes fear, confusion, and often a sense of helplessness. It is a journey that touches not only those living with it but also their families, communities, and faith. In the face of a society that frequently marginalises and misunderstands those affected by dementia, this book provides a powerful counter-narrative. It shows how, through a Christian lens, dignity, meaning, and belonging can be found even in the midst of forgetfulness and loss.

Wendy Gleadle's reflections in Part I draw richly on personal stories, theological insights, and creative approaches, demonstrating how individuals with dementia can remain spiritually connected and vibrant. Her emphasis on God's unfailing presence reminds us that faith is not bound to cognitive capacity but resides in the depths of our being, where God's love continues to sustain us.

In Part II, Frances Attwood challenges churches to see themselves as active agents of God's love, uniquely positioned to provide support and community for families living with dementia. With practical wisdom and inspiring examples, she illustrates how the church can respond to the spiritual, social, and emotional needs of these families, fostering spaces of hope and healing.

This book is not just a resource for those directly impacted by dementia but a call to action for the wider church. It invites us to reconsider how we think about personhood, community, and care. It challenges us to live out our faith in ways that reflect God's love for all, especially the vulnerable and forgotten.

Dementia, God, and the Church is a reminder that even in the most difficult of journeys, there is hope. For those grappling with the realities of dementia, it offers encouragement and comfort. For caregivers, it provides guidance and affirmation. For the church, it presents an opportunity to embody Christ's compassion in new and transformative ways.

May this book inspire all who read it to embrace the journey of dementia not as a path of despair but as a sacred pilgrimage – a journey towards understanding, connection, and the abiding presence of God.

The Revd Professor John Swinton
Professor in Practical Theology and Pastoral Care
University of Aberdeen

Introduction

Dementia: offering a positive outlook

Therefore we do not lose heart. Though outwardly we are wasting away, yet inwardly we are being renewed day by day.
2 CORINTHIANS 4:16

Dementia is one of today's most feared health conditions, not only because of the devastating effect it can have, but also because of the myths and misunderstandings that contribute to the stigma and isolation people can feel. Many people across society still feel uncomfortable in coping with dementia, only seeing it as a negative and hopeless condition, and this unease is still reflected across much of the contemporary church as well. However, the aim of this book is to show how those living with dementia can still find hope and meaning and to consider how churches can do more to support them and their families.

Before looking at changing attitudes to dementia, it seems appropriate to first briefly set out the medical nature of the condition. The term 'dementia' covers a range of diseases, including Alzheimer's disease, vascular dementia, Lewy body dementia, frontotemporal dementia, and several others. The accepted medical definition across the spectrum is summarised in this description from the World Health Organization:

> *Dementia is a syndrome that can be caused by a number of diseases which over time destroy nerve cells and damage the brain, typically leading to deterioration in cognitive function (i.e. the ability to process thought) beyond what might be expected from the usual consequences of biological ageing. While consciousness is not affected, the impairment in cognitive function is commonly accompanied, and occasionally preceded, by changes in mood, emotional control, behaviour, or motivation.*[1]

This kind of definition has led many to conclude that dementia destroys the inner self and leaves a shell that looks like the person but is no longer the person. If the ability to be self-aware or to relate to others is missing, then personhood is lost. In other words, the symptoms of dementia make them into non-persons. If memories are crucial to our sense of self, then losing memory leads to the question, 'How can we be ourselves, when we have no idea who we are?' While the great strength of western medicine may be its ability to scrutinise and analyse distinct symptoms, it often fails to look at the person holistically. Until the 1990s the future for people living with dementia was miserable, as there was little alternative to the medical model of care, where the person was looked after in a mainly depersonalised way. For a long time, this 'medical model' has held sway and the heart of people's fears has been of losing their memory and, in so doing, losing themselves.

However, 'rementing', the phenomenon where occasionally the person lost to their dementia suddenly regains cognitive ability, especially during their final days or hours, has now been studied by a medical research team, who have reported that 'unexpected lucidity, especially around the time of death, challenges current assumptions and highlights the possibility of some return of cognitive function in severe dementia'.[2] This ongoing research by the medical profession themselves is a first indicator that perhaps the loss of all cognition is not inevitable after all. Nevertheless, it could be argued that while medical definitions of dementia are helpful for therapeutic purposes, they are mainly lacking in contributing to a pastoral or theological approach to the condition.

In the last 25 years alternative approaches to the bleak medical viewpoint have been emerging. Tom Kitwood, one of the first to challenge the accepted medical stance with his groundbreaking work in developing person-centred care, argues that because our understanding of dementia has been so grounded in medical science, the person behind the diagnosis has been lost. Those living with dementia are often accepted as no longer being themselves, often to the extent of already being thought of as dead. But Kitwood sees dementia in the context of a person's whole life, their personality, relationships and any other condition. He believes it is crucial to treat each person as an individual and approach them with knowledge of who they are (not who they were).[3]

John Swinton puts this viewpoint precisely:

> *Supporters of this person-centred approach regard personhood in people living with dementia as being concealed rather than lost; they acknowledge personhood in all aspects of care; they ensure personalised care; they offer shared decision-making as long as possible; they interpret behaviour from the person's point of view and personal relationships are prioritised over care tasks.*[4]

Indeed, people living with dementia may behave differently but are still whole people. Gradually, following Kitwood's theories of person-centred care, other viewpoints have been emerging – they are all hopeful and encouraging, but offer quite a broad and even bewildering range of opinions.

John Killick is a proponent of rewriting the usual negative words in describing those living with dementia. Instead of 'wandering' he suggests 'sightseeing'; instead of 'aggressive' he suggests 'lets her needs be known'; instead of 'agitated' he uses 'spirited'; and instead of 'dementia' he prefers 'no worries for tomorrow'. He points out that the 'challenging behaviour' so often discussed actually means they challenge us by the way they act. He stresses, 'It is vital to realise they do not choose to behave in this way, they are reacting to the inadequate way we are behaving towards them!'[5]

Some Christian writers and theologians are enriching this person-centred approach by introducing a complete redescription of dementia from a Christian viewpoint. They seek, in light of scripture and Christian tradition, to redescribe actions and situations in ways that reveal hidden meanings and a new understanding. Redescribing dementia in this way draws attention to the significance of the environment, contacts, and beliefs surrounding a person who has been diagnosed with dementia.

A different interpretation of stored memories is that they are largely undamaged and intact, and that this provides a key to unlock people's isolation and ill-being.

Yet another explanation is not that factual information has been forgotten, but that it has not been stored in the first place – people cannot remember the facts, but they can remember the good or traumatic feelings they provoke.

Another point of view is that dementia and non-dementia form a continuum, and that aspects like memory loss are common to many as they age, and we should drop the idea of a distinct before and after, continuing to give as many positive relationship experiences to everyone as possible. Killick suggests this would certainly make for a happier population than the current set-up, and offers a new and uplifting view from someone supporting a loved one living with dementia. He suggests that if you believe in the concept of a soul, then you have to believe that the soul does not get Alzheimer's any more than it gets cancer. Maybe the soul has an awareness of life around it that transcends the body or the ability to communicate. He even wonders poignantly if 'maybe, just maybe, our people have the unique experience of being able to live in two worlds, ours and a freer one that allows them access to insights and awareness we can't even begin to fathom'.[6]

Others believe that memories are not gone but simply inaccessible without some help and that the future of those living with dementia is not based in past memories but on the many present moments in which they now live.

However, in all this wide-ranging and rather confusing debate, perhaps the essence of the Christian message is best expressed by Debbie Thrower, who suggests that while cognitive function may decrease, the essential person remains; in Christian terms, 'as someone made in the image of God, he or she is loved, lovable and infinitely precious'.[7]

This book is written to underline this more positive and hopeful outlook, in particular to those whose Christian faith is being challenged by living with the hard realities of dementia themselves or their partners who suddenly have to change their role to that of carer. Whether you are reading this because you are living with dementia yourself, are caring for someone with the condition, or are wanting to give better support to family, friends, or church members more generally, we hope to demonstrate that while the diagnosis can be devastating, there is another encouraging side to the story of hope and new possibilities.

The two authors are both Anna Chaplains[8] who have been motivated by their own experiences to write about the different ways those living with dementia can still find hope and meaning. The book is in two parts.

The first part, 'Living with God and dementia', by Wendy, includes the realities of living with dementia by writers living with the condition themselves, showing how they have found hope and meaning by experiencing God through their senses, relationships, and creativity. It explores the implications for those losing their cognition if faith is not only cognitive, but an expression of the whole person, including emotions and relationships. Anna Chaplains and others share experiences of how people with even advanced dementia can still experience and worship God. This first part concludes by exploring God's own continuing relationship and communication with those living with dementia.

The second part, 'How can churches better support families living with dementia?' by Frances, explores the current role of churches in caring for the whole family, reaching out to the marginalised and offering hope. It looks at what people living with dementia and their family carers value and what they would like. It explores responses from church leaders who already have a ministry to this group, as well as the hindrances that other churches experience. It concludes with the hope that can be offered to those living with dementia and challenges the church to do more to help those affected by dementia to appreciate God's love and to grow closer to him.

PART I

Living with God and dementia

Wendy Gleadle

1

Living with dementia: the journey begins

We are hard pressed on every side, but not crushed; perplexed, but not in despair.
2 CORINTHIANS 4:8

It is all too easy to imagine the heartache and dread a diagnosis of any dementia must bring. But of course, only those actually living with dementia can really know how it feels. Missed hospital appointments and keys left in strange places give way to more crippling incapacities. Ordinary tasks, like going to the shops for a pint of milk, can become insuperable obstacles to getting through the day. Yet just as the fear of what lies ahead is taking hold, friends may drift away, either scared or repelled by the condition. Dementia is accompanied by stigma, and often people become awkward around those with the condition because they fear that person might start to show embarrassing behaviours. Society values competence, intelligence, and independence and devalues those who might be unable to demonstrate these attributes. Consequently, the belief that those living with dementia are losing these abilities can result in their loneliness and isolation.

This chapter explores the experiences of some Christian writers living with the condition themselves. They describe their early reactions to their diagnosis and how they started to adapt to their new way of life. Despite their fluctuating feelings of fear and despair, they also discovered there was still meaning and hope in their relationship with God.

Christine Bryden[1]

Christine originally worked in the pharmaceutical industry, then in publishing in the UK, Holland, and Australia, and finally as a senior executive in the Australian Prime Minister's department, advising the prime minister on science and technology. After some months of headaches, confusion, and difficulties finding her way around, she went to see the doctor. She was subjected to many tests before he bluntly told her that she had dementia, should retire from work immediately, and should not be in any position of authority. She was just 46 years old. This was a devastating diagnosis at this age – surely dementia only happened to much older people? The specialist said in a few years she would need full-time care, and then it would only be a few years until she died. But it has been over 25 years since that awful time, and since that distressing diagnosis she has written several books, countless articles, and has been a worldwide and sought-after speaker on the subject of dementia. Christine is particularly adept at describing the many ways her life was changing in the early stages of her dementia.

> *The complexity of so many things is a source of anguish. Just getting up, how to make a cup of tea, how to go and have a shower, where are my clothes and what shall I wear. I suppose the anguish is because no one seems to realise how difficult everything is. We can be tempted to maintain a cheerful façade, and deny anything is wrong. You may either go along with this and deny dementia, or assume we lack insight and take over our lives. We cannot win. My memory comes and goes, with glimpses of past events or future tasks I wish to do. But I can't*

find the memories when I want to, and I rush to note them down. It feels as if I will forget everything that is not written down.

I realise I now ask the same question again without any awareness of having asked it before. I know it drives others crazy to hear the same thing over and over, but how much worse is it for the person with dementia who knows they have asked you a question, but can't remember the answer? I often ask a question and realise by the expression on the person's face that I have asked this before, probably just a short while ago.

I have also started putting things in the wrong place. This is because I am going to put it somewhere, then something else pops into my head, and I put it down, and of course cannot recall later where it was. I don't hide things on purpose. I can't even remember that I had it in my hand, so I am just as likely to accuse you of taking it and hiding it.

Questions like, 'Do you remember?' fill me with panic. Descriptions of your own recollections are much more helpful, as these give me time to think and may also sometimes trigger my own memory so I can share my feelings with you. Before diagnosis, 'What do you do?' was easy to answer. But now I can't answer that question.

Far more important to Christine is who she is and to know the relationships around her that give her comfort and a sense of support and encouragement. There is such a terrible stigma attached to this condition that no one wants to talk about it. She explains poignantly that people living with dementia struggle to remain 'normal' and pretend they are feeling fine. But actually, they are not. They know what it feels like to be normal, and this is not what it feels like now. She says: *It becomes more difficult to describe how we feel, to get our thoughts in order and actually get the words out so you can understand us.*

In those early days Christine describes how thankful she was to have discovered a new sense of an emotional and spiritual self within her church community. She began to regard cognitive ability as perhaps being less important than an ability to relate to others and to what was giving her a new sense of meaning. However, she was still sometimes overwhelmed by fear as the story of loss of self always seemed to permeate any discussion of dementia.

In all her writing, Christine emphasises that she is an individual, who happens to have a condition of her brain. She found it hard to deal with all the neurologist's medical charts and graphs which she felt denied her of her individuality, and in particular of any credibility as she was still able to write and speak after many years of living with the condition. She explains how easy it is for people to believe the stereotype of dementia – being unable to speak or recognise anyone, and what a constant battle everyone has to overcome the fear of these later stages that are so prominently the picture everyone has of dementia. She so wanted to stress that there is a long journey beforehand, between diagnosis and the end stage, the journey of learning to live with dementia each day. She describes this as travelling a journey deep into the core of their spirit, into the centre of their being, into what truly gives them meaning in life. Her personal reflections show how isolating the diagnosis can be.

> *I lost my circle of friends and colleagues; I felt I had been cast out into the wilderness, abandoned and alone. I became isolated from the world, feeling distant from God. I was in the valley of the shadow of death, and yet I came to realise that God was with me. Despite all that was happening within me, the voice of the psalmist remained true: 'Yet shall I dwell in the house of the Lord my whole life long' (Psalm 23:6). I turned to him in faith, longing to find hope in my suffering, knowing in my soul that 'the steadfast love of the Lord never ceases' (Lamentations 3:22).*

Christine says she and her husband Paul are a team, navigating the unknown. With Paul's help, and her faith as her anchor, she says she has been able to turn the suffering around – the shock, the horror, the fear, the trauma, which was true for a couple of years – to try to use it for God's glory and to benefit the church. Through her talks and her books, she says she hopes she can encourage families of people living with dementia, ministers, and pastoral carers to see dementia through a 'faith lens'. She writes:

> *So, they realise that no matter how severe the dementia, we are fully human and loved by God. We are embodied souls and endowed with the breath of God. We're animated by God. Never will I be an empty shell. As I lose an identity in the world around me, which is so anxious to define me by what I do and say, rather than who I am, I can seek an identity by simply being me, created in the image of God, reflected in the divine and given meaning as a transcendent being.*

This theme of remaining fully human and loved in the eyes of God is a recurring one in all her writing. Through it all, she's come to an understanding that regardless of whether she can continue to speak or how forgetful she becomes, God still knows and loves her. In fact, Christine says in many ways she's more open in her relationship with God now, living with dementia.

> *My prayers are a big muddle, but I'm sure God doesn't mind. Before, my head was full of stuff. Sometimes now (though not always) I can just relax and be with God. I see that as a real gift.*

By speaking in terms of her inner spirit, she touches on the sense of people living with dementia being a sign to others of the quite different values of the kingdom of God. She becomes aware that she can simply 'be' and allow God to work in her journey with dementia. She discovered that within the personal experience of a life lived with dementia, she was travelling towards less of herself and more of God. Christine believes that as her cognition fades, her spirituality can flourish as an important source of her identity.

Doctors don't seem to be able to attribute Christine's current condition to anything other than the fact that she was exceptionally bright prior to diagnosis. But Christine says her Christian faith has been her mainstay. In an interview with the *Church Times* in 2012, she spoke of the difference her Christian faith made to her feelings and outlook of living with dementia:

> *When you become a Christian, it's through a spiritual awakening. It's not through me reading texts and struggling to understand God. It's got nothing to do with thinking. It's a work of God. A friend, who is an Anglican priest, met me each month to pray with me and encourage me in the first months and years. She suggested I write about my feelings and insights, and a book emerged, to be followed by others.*
>
> *To our church families I would say: 'Include us, and remember we are whole human beings, with body, mind, and spirit, just like you. We need to be included in all your acts of worship, including Communion, and to be in fellowship with you. You can bring the Christ-light to us in our time of need.'*
>
> *I would be humbled to be remembered for changing the way people with dementia are respected, included, supported, encouraged, and enabled. I have an eternal life with Christ, so my future is infinite. Yes, this temporal life will end, probably in end-stage dementia, but I pray that Paul and my daughters may even then be able to see Christ in me connecting to the Christ in them.*

Christine's aim throughout all her writing is to reach out and help others to understand the insider's perspective of living with dementia. She challenges the outsider's view of loss of self, as she is discovering that, despite problems with sense of time, recall, and language, she has not lost her sense of self. She continues to say: *I'm still here!*

Jennifer Bute[2]

Jennifer was a Christian missionary doctor in Africa for several years before becoming a senior doctor in a large clinical practice back in the UK, when she began to notice symptoms of dementia in herself. She received her diagnosis of young-onset dementia in 2009.

Jennifer believes her dementia is an opportunity as well as a challenge. It has enabled her to reach out to others who are living with the condition. She believes that 'rejoicing in adversity' is a basic scriptural instruction and that there are many physical and mental benefits in doing so. Now living in a dementia-inclusive village, she feels able to walk this path with many others on the same journey, and encourages them to find joy and know God's love.

Jennifer's early cognitive problems started to affect her work as a doctor. She began to have difficulties recognising patients or remembering what she had to do next. She resigned from her clinical work as soon as she realised that no one could say whether she was – and would continue to be – safe. Her patients meant too much to her to put them at risk.

In a pastoral team meeting at her church, before her diagnosis had been confirmed, someone asked whether it was worth visiting a member of the church who now had dementia, because she wouldn't remember the visit or the visitor. Jennifer thought she couldn't bear to be treated like that when her own condition worsened. She asked to give a talk to the pastoral and staff team, and this was so well received that they had it recorded, and her son set up her own website about dementia, **gloriousopportunity.org.** It includes all sorts of practical suggestions that she has found helpful and which she passes on to others.

She was similarly having problems at home. Her husband would find uncompleted tasks, such as half-ironed shirts or food left in the microwave and half-made marmalade. She couldn't remember her postcode or telephone number and had to write herself detailed instructions of the most basic household jobs. She had to be reminded to cook meals, and once cooked supper twice on the same day. Her symptoms increased and she had auditory and visual hallucinations. Jennifer writes:

> *It was very frightening at first. Scripture refers to a 'sacrifice of praise' – sometimes our hearts overflow with praise but at other times it is a costly choice. In church one day, I told a friend I was unravelling and finding it hard. She said her grandmother unravelled things to make them into new things that were just as useful. This was a real encouragement to me – I felt I might still be of some use after all. Knowing the love of Jesus and the power of the Holy Spirit is my greatest help in living with my dementia. Having dementia has made me realise that God wanted me and not my intellectual ability or position.*

Jennifer passionately believes that people living with dementia should be as important in any church family as anyone else. She is often asked to speak in churches around the country, helping people, including chaplains and others who minister to people living with dementia, to understand it better and to see through the dementia to the person himself or herself and be better able to communicate with them. She sees her dementia as a unique advantage in being able to teach others who are experiencing the same.

Her most important insight about living with dementia is that the person 'inside' remains and can still be reached – even when masked by the condition – and that spirituality rises as cognition becomes limited. She has realised that people often 'reappear', prompted by different stimuli – singing, music, reading scripture. Whatever the medical explanation, these breakthroughs show that the person remains, shut inside and unable to get out.

Recently I had the privilege of visiting Jennifer, and she told me how much she loves the following passage, which she finds so relevant to dementia:

Love never dies. Inspired speech will be over some day... understanding will reach its limit. We know only a portion of the truth, and what we say about God is always incomplete. But when the Complete arrives, our incompletes will be cancelled... We don't yet see things clearly. We're squinting in a fog, peering through a mist. But it won't be long before the weather clears and the sun shines bright! We'll see it all then, see it all as clearly as God sees us, knowing him directly just as he knows us!
1 CORINTHIANS 13:8–10, 12 (MSG)

As well as her Christian reflections and insights on living with dementia, Jennifer has also written of the many practical techniques she uses to adapt to her own cognitive challenges.

I have always been computer-literate so now my computer is my backup brain. I have an online calendar set up for automatic reminders and can be networked with my children's computers, so they always know what I am doing or where I am. Writing notes to myself does not work, as I either forget to read them, do not see them, or cover them up. I leave a card on the floor where I will notice it. I also leave things to post, or take anywhere, by the front door where I can't miss them.

My Alexa device reminds me to take my medication and checks on whether I have. Alexa also reads books, plays me any song or piece of music without my needing to remember the exact details, and answers any question I ask without my having to look it up.

I find shops overwhelming, so I do my shopping online. I cannot remember whether I have eaten or not and writing it down or ticking boxes does not work, as how do I know if I remembered? The only thing that works for me is to either only wash up once a day so I can see which dishes have been used or never put anything away until I go to bed. I decide the day before what to wear and lay it all out on the carpet in order.

> *I cannot work out how to answer my mobile, so I only use it for texts as I cannot understand what people are saying on the phone, but I do use Zoom and Telegram – a video/chat/photo-sharing platform. I am blessed by belonging to a local church. They take me to church and out for meals. I have a card I can give to people which describes who I am, my diagnosis, what I may struggle with, and contact telephone numbers.*

My favourite quote from Jennifer is about the art of *kintsukuroi* – repairing broken pottery with costly gold or silver:

> *The art of kintsukuroi is a wonderful picture to me of how God has poured his love and grace into my life to hold it together, making it more beautiful and giving it greater value.*

It was inspiring to hear of her continuing closeness to God, and my lasting memory of our recent conversation is her belief that it is an honour when God entrusts you with any difficult situation – even dementia.

Robert Davis[3]

Robert was a Baptist minister for many years, and was diagnosed with presenile dementia in 1989 when he was only 52 years old. Interestingly, his writing reflects the more negative reactions of the time before the person-centred approaches were recognised, although he himself derived great comfort and peace from his faith in God.

> *My neurologist was reviewing my medical report. He told me he did not know the cause, but the tests showed a form of presenile dementia. He said the condition was permanent and irreversible. We sat for a moment whilst I digested what he had told me. Then he asked me how I felt about it. I told him, 'I know that the Lord is with me. That knowledge has always given me inner peace. He has always had a purpose for me. I trust that this is part of that purpose.'*

How can I stand to look at this disaster of dementia that medical science predicts will most probably overtake me? If I were not a Christian, I do not know how I could stand it. However, since I am a Christian, I can stand it by looking beyond it – looking beyond and considering the glories of heaven where each one of these things will be gone forever and be replaced by perfection, glory, and joy.

Robert and his wife Betty looked for books and articles to help them understand and prepare for a very bad situation. They found little help. At the time Robert was diagnosed there was little written or understood about the devastating condition. He felt it was a hidden world, because the people concerned have lost their ability to communicate. Robert was determined to be the voice for all those victims who had lost their ability to communicate even before anyone knew what was bringing on all these distressing changes. Even as his own ability to communicate was rapidly deteriorating, he wanted to give the concerned families some insight as to the 'blackness' and 'lost' feelings of those living with dementia by writing about his own difficulties as his journey with Alzheimer's started. He also wanted to help those who might be questioning God's provisions, Christ's power to give comfort, the joy Christ pours on the helpless, and the mystery of suffering.

I can no longer remember a list that goes above five items. I sometimes become lost and confused, even in familiar stores. I can become lost in a motel room and not even able to find the bathroom door. My mind has become a sieve that can only catch and hold random things. Previously I could remember accurately any place I'd ever been. Now all these pictures are gone – I cannot even remember what my mother looked like.

Suddenly his wife Betty was not simply the wife he had loved, but also his caregiver. She had to guide him through daily living as he had become a care receiver, unable to fully care for himself. When he realised overwhelming fears coming on, he had to physically move to break the spell. He would take a shower, ride his exercise bike, or go for a walk. After such stimulation, he found the spell was broken and he was saved from his internal torment. Since this worked so well for him, Robert wondered if the ceaseless walking and wandering of Alzheimer's patients was their effort to raise themselves out of the agony of their own fears.

Modern music with its heavy beat gave him discomfort and headaches. But then he found his old collection of records, including some simple old hymns. This music really spoke to him. The new music seemed irrelevant, but the old music was spiritually refreshing. Robert wondered if others living with Alzheimer's disease would have the same reaction.

> *I am becoming more convinced of the importance of humour and laughter. Laughter, intense laughing, is what separates us from other life forms on our planet. Animals can be happy, but they can't laugh out loud until their sides hurt. People living with dementia can laugh that hard, but sadly they seldom do. We should share, encourage, and point out all moments of joy and glee to one another, especially to people living with dementia whose lives are too much defined by sadness. I'm beginning to wonder if the journey that takes me away from reality into the blackness of the blank, emotionless, unmoving Alzheimer's stare is in reality a journey into the richest depths of God's love that few have experienced on earth.*

Then came the cruellest blow of all. The personal relationship he had had with the Lord seemed to have gone. He could not feel any peace or joy. For months he could not read or pray properly. His thoughts were permanently, *Why, God, why?* When he turned to his Bible to try to get some explanation, he realised fully what his loss of reading ability meant.

But then Betty recorded long passages of scripture that he could listen to at night when unable to sleep. God's word, combined with hearing her familiar voice, was both soothing and comforting for him. They went on a trip and at last he found some respite in the ever-changing scenery and the wonder of God's creation. But at night the darkness always returned.

> *But then one night, a light seemed to fill my very soul. The holy presence of Christ came to me. He spoke to my spirit and said, 'Take my peace. Stop your struggling. Relax and stop desperately searching for answers. I will hold you.' His love overwhelmed me, and moment by moment I can now take his peace and use his strength to simply live. This experience finally lifted the dark veil. It did not make my brain whole again. I am still living with disability and will continue to become more dependent as my disease progresses. But now I am assured that I am not alone. As Isaiah 43:2 reminds us: 'When you pass through the waters, I will be with you; and when you pass through the rivers, they will not sweep over you.'*

* * *

Christine, Jennifer, and Robert are uplifting examples of people whose dementia journey has been made so much easier to bear by their ongoing relationship with God. But, of course, when someone is diagnosed with dementia, it affects so many other people too – their partners, children, wider family, and friends. In particular, for those married or in a long-term relationship, it is a devastating change for the partner who quite quickly becomes the carer instead of an equal partner. And it is to their experiences that we turn in the next chapter.

2

Living with dementia: the shared journey

It's not how much you do, but how much love you put into the doing.
Mother Teresa[1]

Dementia is a complex, unpredictable, and progressive condition, so caring for a person living with dementia is often unlike caring for someone with any other illness. For anyone who loves and cares for someone living with dementia, their decline can appear as nothing less than a tragedy. 'They are caring for someone who is experiencing the opposite of remembering. It is an experience of unremembering and unmaking.'[2]

One of the most difficult things about caring for a person living with dementia can be the range of emotions experienced. The carer may feel frustrated, exhausted, or burnt out. They may be angry and may wonder, 'Why me?' They might also feel isolated and cut off from the world. It is common for a carer to feel lonely, especially as their relationship with the person living with dementia changes. There may be times when they worry that they are only caring for them out of a sense of duty. Or they may feel they no longer love or even like the person they are caring for. They might also feel grief – as if they are losing the person they once knew. There may be days when they feel they can cope well and other days when they feel that they can't. There may be some parts of caring that they find easy to manage, but other things that are difficult. These are all common reactions to caring for a person with dementia, and everyone will experience caring in their own way.

Carers have to cope not only with their changing role, but often also with the unhelpful responses of others. As one carer wrote:

> *It is no help to me when well-intentioned friends extend me the shallow counsel to 'look on the bright side', to 'accept what God wills' or to 'learn the lessons of this journey'. This deflection from reality is usually for the sake of the good-hearted dispenser of these sayings rather than for me, the care-giver!*[3]

Here are a few more actual responses from carers themselves to their new role:[4]

> *He is leaving me behind. I don't know where he is going, and I don't understand the language or the country where he dwells. Try as hard as I may to pull him back from the edge of the abyss called dementia, he is leaving me anyway. Spectacularly, once, after I'd screamed at him for some perceived misdemeanour, I told him it wasn't him I was mad at but the illness. The next day he said, 'You know when you said it wasn't me you were mad with, but the illness?' 'Yes', I replied, expecting some criticism. 'Well,' he continued, 'I found that really helpful'. This illness is depriving both of us of so much. It is not possible for two to survive in this relationship without some massive realignment of the boundaries. The re-thinking or re-definition that is required takes enormous energy, as the carer's needs are superseded by the needs of the sufferer. Even if it had been an equal relationship, the carer becomes the controller of the*

other: this seems necessary, because otherwise the dementia controls. The dementia is not the person. [A. Young]

I think the early days of his illness were worse than when the Alzheimer's became more advanced. Getting him ready to bring him to church on a Sunday was difficult. This had been the pattern of his life and was important to him. It hurt me to see this man who had been such a robust preacher sitting at the back, picking threads off his hat. I felt angry that so few people talked to him or even acknowledged his presence. [H. Robinson]

She was admitted to hospital having had a fall. There was no medical need for her to stay very long, but social services were slow to organise her follow-up care, and she ended up staying for five weeks, during which time she deteriorated beyond repair. What amazes me, in retrospect, is that the nurses and doctors seemed oblivious to the terrible drama unfolding before their eyes. Not one person sat us down and talked to us about what her sudden plunge into advanced dementia might mean. Not one person gave us any recognition that suddenly our mother had been taken from us as surely as if she had died in her hospital bed. Why was there so little expert recognition of dementia, in the care of the elderly ward of all places? [L. Whitman]

How does the wife in her 40s ever come to terms with the loss of a beloved partner? Gone are the shared memories, happiness, future you had planned together. What remains? Coping with the practical aspects of bringing up a family, caring for a husband, planning for a future you don't want to happen. Having to bear the hurt of friends and family who vanish into thin air. Finding the strength to battle for advice on caring, support, benefits, and services available, none of which ever catch up with your needs. This is a nightmare nothing could have ever prepared you for. [S. Nurock]

I did not see myself as the carer. I saw myself more as her protector and perhaps the manager of the care she was getting. I got tired and angry, and at times I saw myself as coping or not coping with the stress of caring, and as being active or passive in relation to the challenges: as a saint, I sense I am doing the right thing; as a sinner, that I am not up to the challenge. As a hero, I have a sense I am making a difference; as a martyr, though, I am resigned to my fate. The comments of others would reinforce these states of mind: 'I do admire your courage': I was definitely heroic! – 'I don't know how you do it' – martyrdom awaits! [T. Dartington]

The illustrations above show how carers and partners can feel fear and apprehension as they grieve for lost opportunities and try to adapt to a completely new way of life. But carers can also find hope and positivity in their situation, as the following carer suggests:

It may seem strange to speak of the gift of my mother's dementia, and I certainly only refer to it as – in some ways – a gift to me. I cannot but believe that for her, much of the time, it was dreadful. But I learned so much, especially in her last year or so – about being less cerebral, about what that word grace could mean, about the loving kindness of the care home staff. The greatest gift was that my intimate connection with my mother's slow dying gave me in a way a chance to rehearse my own approach to death, as a traveller with the person dying, as a witness that it can be a serene and peaceful journey, and that it may hold within it 'something more'.[5]

There is no training for dementia care and no pattern to follow, because each case is different: a mixture of the condition itself and the personality of the individual. It's a journey into the unknown, and the most important aspect of care is the love the caregiver has for the person living with dementia.

For example, John Zeisel, an internationally renowned expert on dementia care and innovative treatments, makes the fundamental point that the person living with dementia is still a person, to whom we continue to relate, though it is a different and changing relationship. He advocates that carers should be able to continue including the one they care for as they continue to mix in society – in churches, museums, and theatres, among other places. He points out that most people live with their condition for over a decade, and that for much of that time they can function with less help than most people think, can still enjoy themselves, and even learn new things. In particular, he believes that the people who care for them can maintain positive relationships and share vibrant memories for much of the course of the illness through photos, music, art, personal stories, and visits to community and cultural events.

Zeisel further offers some key pieces of advice for partners when things get difficult:

- *Live within your own capabilities and limits.* How much caregiving and treatment are you honestly able to take on?

- *Don't push the limits as far as they will go.* Many partners will say, 'It's not bad enough yet.' But the measure of when to act is when it is best for both the person living with dementia and their partner.

- *Establish your own life and rhythm.* Start new skills or hobbies, or a new schedule with time for yourself.

- *Establish a lifeline or two.* Your situation is trying, and will become more trying as the condition progresses. Whom can you 'vent' to? Can you find a formal support group who are dealing with similar issues?

- *Learn to say, 'Please help me.'* In order to take care of yourself, learn to say, 'Please help me.'

- *Learn to give up.* In this journey there is a point when you can't go further, at least at that moment. Learn to do what you can do and be ready to drop it when it becomes overwhelming. Be open to exploring the idea of carers coming in, or a care home for your loved one.[6]

To close this chapter, I have slightly paraphrased Henri Nouwen's thought-provoking paragraph about being a carer:

> *To care one must offer one's own vulnerable self to others as a source of healing. As long as we think that caring means only being nice and friendly to frail old people, paying them a visit, bringing them a flower, or offering them a ride, we are apt to forget how much more important it is for us to be willing and able to be present to those we care for. Only when we enter into solidarity with them and speak out of common experience, can we truly engage with those living with dementia.*[7]

3

Dementia and religious beliefs

My soul thirsts for God, for the living God.
PSALM 42:2

It is thought-provoking to realise that the spiritual life continues for people who no longer have the cognitive ability to do spirituality in the way we normally identify it. This spiritual sense of meaning is part of what it is to be human – it is part of who we are. We can support those living with dementia by discerning their spiritual needs, even into advanced stages of the condition. It is a highly significant element in helping them to cope with this difficult and painful experience. While cognitive abilities may continue to be lost, the search for a sense of meaning at the very core of our being remains, even for those with advanced dementia. 'This deep level of connection beyond language is profound and connects with the spiritual and ultimately, with God.'[1]

Spirituality plays an essential role in the lives of older adults and is an important factor in health, well-being, and preserved cognitive function as adults age. A study published in the National Library of Medicine systematically reviewed the literature examining the effects of religion and spirituality on health outcomes, such as cognitive functioning, coping strategies, and quality of life in people living with dementia. They showed that in participants who maintained their religious practices and social interactions, their cognitive disorders tended to reduce or stabilise. In addition, expressions of spiritual practices or faith in daily life enabled people to develop coping strategies to help accept their condition, maintain their relationships, maintain hope, and find meaning in their lives, thereby improving their quality of life.[2]

Engaging in these activities helps instil some sense of control over one's current life as people living with dementia experience loss of independence and functional decline. Involving them with familiar sources of meaning and connection is reaffirming – rituals for Christians living with dementia can include candles, mealtime grace, bedtime prayers, biblical texts, prayer books, and religious symbols, such as rosary beads, a crucifix, or a cross. In the earlier stages of dementia, Christians can still find peace and hope in practising their usual religious activities, such as reading their Bible, prayer, and going to church services. These are not so much significant in themselves but as a means and expression of relationship with God and other believers.

However, as their condition progresses, they may find it increasingly difficult to practise their religion in these cognitive ways of their earlier days. Attendance at church services may be particularly difficult for them. Unpredictable, informal departures from the normal service may be confusing. If the songs are unfamiliar, the Christian living with dementia can feel lost and disconnected from God's closeness and may well become spiritually discouraged. For those whose dementia is gradually making participation in traditional worship inaccessible, other ways need to be found to help them to grow in their faith and experience the presence of God. They still need to find meaning in their life through other areas that remain available to them, through which God can reach them, including relationships, the arts, creation, and creativity (which we will explore in chapters 5 and 6).

In the Christian context, a faith commitment is expressed by being a follower of Jesus, with its accompanying understanding of being in a personal relationship with God. This suggests a trustful relationship, obedient following of God in Christ, and meanings and values which are deep-rooted in their sense of identity. These are still at the core of a Christian who is facing the particular challenges of dementia. Indeed, 'there is a sense that dementia, in stripping away some of our traditional methods for "doing business with God" has the potential to take us to a place where it is easier for God to do business with us'.[3]

'Tricia Williams writes of two people living with dementia who bear this out, Alice and Ron. She quotes Alice:

> *The less I have, the more amazed I am at what God does with it. Whereas, when I was working, I thought some of it was me. I thought God had given me many gifts and I was quite clever! But now I realise everything that happens is of God. So, in a sense, I'm closer to God now because there's less of me.*

This will resonate with the many Christians who, having been filled with the Holy Spirit, continually pray, 'Less of me, and more of you.' Alice's inference is that the reducing of her cognition has brought her increased awareness of her dependence on God. The more the dementia symptoms were increasing, the more intense her spiritual life was becoming. When Alice was further asked about her faith, she said:

> *It's not a work, it's not a doing. It's a relationship to Someone that I love and who loves me. I know that God is always with me, because He always has been, and I know that there's nothing that can ever separate me from him.*

Ron said:

> *The joy of being born again is always there. You can't separate one or the other... and so I'll never lose that joy, even if I have lost my memory.*[4]

His confidence that he would never lose the joyful sense of God's presence in his life was striking. Alice and Ron are just two examples of people living with dementia who no longer need the trappings of religion to still experience the joy of God being with them. It certainly seems that being in a faithful relationship with God takes priority over the 'doing' of religious practices.

My thoughts so far have assumed that the person living with dementia is a believer and/or a church member when they are first diagnosed. But what of those who have no Christian beliefs? Is it possible to share the gospel with someone who will not be able to remember what has been said? Is there a different way of bringing Jesus to those who forget so quickly? Is simply sharing God's love sufficient without a rational explanation being given? If the good news is to be proclaimed to those who are living with dementia and those who care for them, vague gestures of concern will not do.

There are four typical 'models' in which the Christian faith can be taught and experienced, but possibly only the fourth is applicable for those who are living with dementia.

1. A *traditional* model, in which memory is central in placing us in a shared tradition, and which therefore progressively excludes those whose memory is vanishing.

2. An *open to God* model, which envisages each individual as being moved by the Spirit into an ever-richer enjoyment of God's fellowship, but which often runs counter to the experience of those who are living with dementia.

3. A *growth* model, which envisages the individual as continuously journeying towards full spiritual maturity – again, this seems counter to the experienced diminishment of those whose cognition is lessening.

4. A *remembered by God* model, which seems to be the only theological model which captures the 'good news' for the person living with dementia, stressing that we are unconditionally accepted by God, regardless of our ability to make a recognisable response to him.

The attractions of this final model are clear, and some version of it underpins the majority of pastoral theology developed in response to dementia. It gives a simple, clear message of hope and comfort, both for the individual living with dementia and for those close to them, which does not depend upon any doctrinal belief or subtlety beyond the sense of a present, caring God. A true account of God should be one that begins from this point: that God is present in extremity, and will be there at the very moments when the person's cognition is failing.[5]

There are some who wonder whether trying to share the gospel with someone living with dementia is pointless. They suggest we should save the gospel for those who can comprehend and remember. But quite a different story emerges when talking to Christians who are caring for people in varying stages of dementia. Many carers and supporters are discovering that even those most lost in their dementia will respond with a smile or tears to a hymn, prayer, or embrace from a Christian carer. When I was in touch with other Anna Chaplains, several talked of people who started their dementia journey with no belief in God, but seemed to gain a heightened sense of dependency and need, and recognised that God could and would meet those needs in ways neither they nor their carers could explain.

For an atheist or agnostic person who has advanced dementia, to be told that God loves them may not come as a surprise. They may have forgotten their years of rejecting God. Their bitterness at their condition may be lost. Their life in the present is entirely dependent. They are now living in the present moment that God can fill, and they can be told of God's goodness in that moment. Many of the older people who have no faith now will still have a residual memory of school hymns, old choruses, and readings. But for those with little or no faith, storytelling using a calming, multisensory approach can be helpful, which can include talking about Jesus in a simple, straightforward way. 'Tricia Williams writes of several people living with dementia who have responded to being told that Jesus loves, forgives, and accepts them, one being Elsie, an older lady with no known pre-dementia faith commitment, who responded with a joyful 'Does he?'[6]

But what of those whose dementia has become so advanced that they no longer even remember Jesus? What happens if you cannot confess the Lord with your mouth? How can you call upon the name of the Lord and be saved if you have forgotten who the Lord is? What does it mean to be a disciple when you don't know who Jesus is or you have forgotten who he is?

John Swinton addresses these questions when he recalls his early days as a mental health chaplain working with people living with severe dementia. He discovered that people would very often 'spring into life' when asked to pray the Lord's Prayer, their words clear and coherent, quite unlike their usual lack of communicational responses. He writes:

> *When I offered people the Eucharist, their bodies reached out and responded even when their minds no longer seemed able to grasp the intellectual complexities of the practice. When we greeted one another with the peace of Christ, people would respond and embrace, even if only for a brief moment, in ways that they simply didn't respond in other contexts. As we sang 'When I survey the wondrous cross', the movement of my emotions towards tears was often matched by the tears of the worshippers who had forgotten so much but still seemed to remember Jesus. My medical colleagues told me that it was nothing other than procedural memory: the product of long-term memories of skills that were well learned and ingrained into people's memories in ways that more recent memories were not. Technically, from the perspective of their analytical tools, they may have been correct. But I was never fully convinced.*[7]

Since those early days of ministry, Swinton has come to believe that we are deeply embedded in our memories not just because we can recall them, but because we *are* them. Even when, in terms of cognition and recall, we seem to have forgotten everything, we still remain held in our memories. There is an endurance of bodily memory that surpasses recall and potentially acts as a powerful channel for knowing Jesus even if one has forgotten who Jesus is. But as Swinton points out:

> *Memory on its own in whatever form is not enough to enable us to worship well. Worship, for all people, is something we participate in through the power of the Spirit with a view to encountering God and offering God the best that we can. If people living with advanced dementia have forgotten how to pray, that is nothing more than a reminder of the condition of all of us. Theological reflection on worshipping with people who live with advanced dementia helps us to see that Christian education is life together. Ministering with such people brings to the fore some of the complexities of what the church is and what it is intended to do as an educational institution.*[8]

The challenges that all this brings to the local church in their responsibility to offer support, understanding, and care to those living with dementia is addressed by Frances in the second part of this book.

4

Faith is not just cognitive: it is a response of the whole person

The only thing that counts is faith expressing itself through love.
GALATIANS 5:6

Just how important is it to have mental capacity to know and appreciate God? Can faith express itself in more ways than only cognitive, including our feelings, will, and other aspects of our personalities? These are the fundamental questions to be addressed as we support those whose cognition is declining.

In the 16th century, John Calvin, the French theologian, pastor, and leading reformer during the Protestant Reformation, seemed to have a cognitive view of our knowledge of God: 'Nearly all the wisdom we possess, true and sound, consists of two parts: the knowledge of God and of ourselves.' It has been suggested that Protestant Christianity has fostered a rational understanding of what it means to be a Christian. While Calvin's own knowledge of God was relational, leading to reverence and love, some of Calvin's followers were much given to rational arguments which reduced faith and made it less personal and more intellectual. However, in the 17th century, Blaise Pascal, the French philosopher, said, 'the heart has its reasons, of which reason knows nothing', arguing for the knowledge of God through faith and experience, not just intellectual argument as emphasised by Enlightenment thinkers.

Today, in the west, the logical, rational thinking of the Enlightenment is still ingrained in how we understand the meaning of faith. Even as Christian believers, many of us assume that our cognitive capacities demonstrate our humanity and worth. But suddenly being faced with a diagnosis of dementia, for ourselves or a loved one, leads us to ask ourselves about the nature of our identity and faith.

In a recent conversation John Swinton unpicked this interesting conundrum for me. He suggested that 'this assumption that faith is something that goes on in your mind, and that to have a relationship with God you have to know who you are, know who God is, and be aware of where you are, all stems from the traditions of reform Protestants. But not every denomination thinks that way.' This led me to realise that my own biases stem from a lifetime of belonging to churches with an intellectual approach to both belief and spirituality, and I wonder if my present membership of a more charismatic Baptist church is making it easier for me to accept the argument that emotions and senses are as central to faith as cognitions.

Pondering on this led me to question whether the roots of understanding about the importance of feelings might go back to the very beginnings of our faith in the Old Testament, where knowing God is fundamental, but where this 'knowing' is more than intellectual? In Deuteronomy 6:5, the command is: 'Love the Lord your God with all your heart and with all your soul and with all your strength.' In Hebrew thought, the heart was the seat of the will and mental capacity (rather than of feeling), the soul was the seat of desire and feeling, and strength was physical ability. So, you are being commanded to love God with your whole person. In the gospels, the word 'mind' is added to complete this idea of the whole person, as by then the Greek word for heart was more linked with feelings and emotions. As one commentator writes about Matthew 22:37: 'Heart, soul and mind are not different parts of man, but different ways of thinking about the whole man in his relation to God; no clear distinction can be drawn between them.'[1]

In other words, the biblical understanding of knowing God has always been the whole person. Jesus often referred to the disciples as his friends, implying emotions and relationship, and Paul talks about a personal knowledge of Christ (Philippians 3:8–10). This would seem to mean that the biblical understanding of knowing God and responding to God is always the whole person and not something merely intellectual or cognitive, though that is included.

Perhaps the mainstream of Christian thinking has always included emotion, will, and personal experience along with reason in our response to God, but maybe our surrounding cognitively aware culture has influenced the contemporary church's way of thinking. For example, much of the church seems unaware that those living with dementia can still experience faith through their emotions and senses, despite their increasing lack of cognition. Paul tells us that the body is a temple of the Holy Spirit (1 Corinthians 6:19), which in turn means we experience God's presence in our bodily senses – and people with diminished cognitive functioning maintain sensory capacities, some even becoming heightened as the condition progresses. 'Gentle touches, glimpses of beauty, sounds of music, the fragrance of flowers, the taste of familiar food – these become expressions of the Word made flesh within the experience of people living with dementia. Abstract thoughts vanish and words disappear, but God's incarnate presence remains.'[2]

When considering how God may interact with a person living with dementia, we should remember that conversion in the Bible is not primarily a change in articulate knowledge. Rather, it is a change in relationship; it is a change of 'being born again', in the words of Jesus to Nicodemus (John 3:1–15); it is a change of status from enemy to adopted child (Galatians 4:5; Ephesians 1:5). It is fundamental to realise that the relationship is initiated by God, or, as Karl Barth said, 'God has found a way to us.' For each individual, whether or not they are living with dementia, their knowledge of God is shaped and filled out by God.[3]

Jesus says we are to come to him as children (Matthew 18:3; Luke 18:17), which speaks both of childlike dependence and undeveloped cognitive ability. Coming to Jesus is always expressed as a work of the Holy Spirit in ways that exclude self-will and cognition. If Jesus came to seek and save the lost, how does this work for a person living with dementia? A good example is the way Jesus responded to the demon-possessed man in the region of the Gerasenes (Luke 8:26–39). The man was not living with dementia, but was without relationships and cognitively deficient. Jesus did not call on him to repent and believe, rather he dealt with his immediate needs and problems. The man ended up in his right mind and at Jesus' feet. His restoration was completely dependent on the grace of Jesus, not through any cognitive understanding of his own. Similarly, those living with dementia do not need cognitive understanding to experience the loving touch of the Holy Spirit.

Christine Bryden believes her lived experience of dementia is part of the diversity of God's creation, and that differing cognitive capacities within the church are simply a reflection of God's likeness. She suggests that it is through the Holy Spirit's power that we are in communion with the church and with God, and that this overrides the necessity for cognition, because it is a spiritual communion. Christine has written at length about her faith sustaining her, and as she finds it increasingly difficult to communicate, it will not only be her own faith, but her own community of faith that will sustain her.

A great strength of Christianity is the community, and from a faith perspective dementia provides the opportunity to connect deeply with each other, until quite late in the condition. Bishop Kenneth Carder suggests that faith communities have a special opportunity to broaden and enhance 'brain health' by affirming the importance of belonging, self-worth, and meaning as components of health.[4] Faith communities provide a broader lens through which to view persons and diseases. We are more than our brains, our memories, our capacities. We are beloved children of God, made in the divine image, with infinite worth and dignity, whatever our capacities. Faith communities need to embody the components of total health and brain health – belonging, worth, meaning, hope, and love. Those living with dementia in such communities can still enjoy all these components with their senses and emotions, regardless of their cognitive ability.

Jennifer Bute told me that it was knowing God in her life that gave her joy – regardless of the restrictions dementia was placing upon her. She believes that as her cognition becomes more limited, she is more aware of spiritual things, possibly because, as cognition decreases, inhibitions and social assumptions are also removed. She said her dementia has greatly deepened her relationship with God.

The words of Alice and Ron, quoted in chapter 3, echo this belief that for people living in various stages of dementia, their faith and appreciation of God's presence are expressed through their feelings and emotions, even though they are losing their cognitive abilities. In John Killick's view the big question is: 'Does dementia have the capacity to engender change in the spiritual realm as well as in the physical and mental? Perhaps it does. It may even be the case that the very decline of reasoning ability releases in some individuals a new capacity for spiritual development.'[5]

John Swinton reminded me that the writer to the Hebrews describes faith as 'confidence in what we hope for and assurance about what we do not see' (Hebrews 11:1). That doesn't mean 'know as much as possible and then you will know who God is'. It is something else – it is recognising that there is a mystery in the midst of what it means to know God. The letter of 1 John 4:8 says that 'God is love'. Love is not an idea or something that you know in your mind, it is something you know with the whole of who you are. So, when it comes to people with advanced dementia still living in the love of God, it doesn't have to be named, and the reason for that is simply that love is a way of being with somebody; it is a feeling that does not need to be analysed. The scripture says that the Spirit 'intercedes for us through wordless groans' (Romans 8:26). The very essence of who God is speaks in a way that we can't understand, we can only live into it, and this applies to all believers, whether or not they are living with dementia.

Henri Nouwen expresses perfectly the possibility of emptying our minds from all thoughts in order to prepare our innermost being as the home for God who wants to dwell in us. And isn't 'emptying our minds' exactly what dementia is doing to those who are living with it?

> *The Jesus Prayer, or any other prayer form, is meant to be a help to gently empty our minds from all that is not God, and offer all the room to him and him alone. But that is not all. Our prayer becomes a prayer of the heart when we have localized in the centre of our inner being the empty space in which our God-filled mind can descend and vanish, and where the distinctions between thinking and feeling, knowing and experience, ideas and emotions are transcended, and where God can become our host. 'The Kingdom of God is within you', Jesus said (Luke 17:21). When we empty our minds from all thoughts and our hearts from all experiences, we can prepare in the centre of our innermost being the home for the God who wants to dwell in us. Then we can say with St. Paul, 'I live now not with my own life but with the life of Christ who lives in me' (Galatians 2:20). And then we can realise that it is not we who pray, but the Spirit of God who prays in us.*[6]

5

Dementia and relationships

Dear friends, let us love one another, for love comes from God.
1 JOHN 4:7

Human beings are created for relationship. The second chapter of the Bible tells us that it's not good for man to be alone (see Genesis 2:18). We are created for relationship with God and with others, we were created to love and be loved. We are not created to be alone. As human beings we are dependent, loved, and relational. All these truths remain constant throughout our entire lives; they are not dependent on our cognition or ability, but they are who God has created us to be. Nevertheless, it can be a challenge for others in society to realise they can reach out and befriend those living with dementia, in particular those living in care homes.

The care home where I served as Anna Chaplain recently had an open morning. They advertised widely on social media and on posters around the town, while I emailed everyone on our church mailing list and announced the event during a church service. On the day itself a good number of residents' relatives, our local MP, and a couple of local press came, but only one person not actually associated with the care home attended!

My initial feelings of disappointment at the poor attendance from the local community led me to question this lack of interest. Perhaps this was just one small illustration of how those living with dementia are the marginalised in our modern society? Certainly, the subject of whether they receive justice in our culture has been questioned widely in the media. A BBC News article quoted one carer saying: 'Having to look after someone with dementia is one of the loneliest things in the world that you can do.'[1] A subsequent newspaper article stated that 32 day centres had been closed in three years, and that these statistics coincide with thousands of those living with dementia ending up in accident-and-emergency departments over the same period. This must be devastating for vulnerable pensioners and is pushing families to breaking point.

But perhaps the tendency for those living with dementia to be marginalised starts nearer to home than at the national level. In local communities, people with advancing dementia are often essentially housebound or hidden away in care homes, where they are effectively removed from their community life and easily forgotten. The whole experience can be painfully lonely for both the one with the condition and their partner. To paraphrase a Nouwen meditation: 'Such sidelining can only exacerbate not so much the condition itself, but the accompanying feelings of being useless, worthless, unappreciated, and unloved.'[2]

This whole situation could and should be completely turned around by offering relationship and friendship. Relationship is still reachable for anyone living with dementia and remains one of the most important things we can do to support them and share God's love with them. Kenneth Carder proposes that mystery is the appropriate place to begin when relating to people living with dementia. This approach 'sees the extensive disability and profound advancing illness as a mystery and not as a problem to be fixed or controlled. It doesn't treat them as fundamentally needy, miserable or pitiable. They are people whose lives are to be entered, celebrated, explored and appreciated.'[3]

If those living with dementia are 'loved, lovable and infinitely precious', as Debbie Thrower so poignantly describes them, it can be argued they will need and value relationships, both with others and with God.[4] One definition of being a person is not in terms of what you can do, but in terms of relationship. Personhood is not an individual achievement, but a gift of community, and it can be argued that individuals are moulded by the relationships that occur as they participate in any form of community. Gerda Saunders, who herself is living with dementia, suggests that 'we are not born with a self that merely has to unfold through the years to reveal our true being, but our self is rather brought into being by the people we encounter on our life path'.[5] Nouwen adds perceptively to this need for community:

> *Life is full of gains and losses, joys and sorrows, ups and downs – but we do not have to live it alone. The wounds of our individual lives, which seem intolerable when lived alone, become sources of healing when we live them as part of a fellowship of mutual care.*[6]

At this point, it should be stressed that it is not necessary for body and soul to be perfectly well to render someone a whole person. A person living with dementia is not 'less whole' than others, for personhood is not lost when cognitive powers fail. It is sad that healthy people so often refer to those living with dementia as 'half persons' or 'bodies still alive after the mind has died'. While dementia may significantly affect a personality, it does not alter the fact they are still persons. They may behave differently, but they are still whole people, made in God's image. Dementia may compromise the awareness of the self, but it does not diminish the self.

'Memory Bridge' is a website dedicated to new ways of relating to people living with dementia. Its founder, Michael Verde, has kindly given us permission to quote at length from it:

> *What bridges people with and without dementia to each other is the spirit. Some people will understand that spirit as the Holy Spirit. Some people will not relate to that term, often because*

it sounds too religious to them. We offer one central metaphor, a Bridge, and several allied metaphorical expressions – Letting Go, Letting In, and Letting Be, for example – but other than those ideas to jumpstart the conversation, Memory Bridge is better understood as a space of potentiality and not as a philosophy or method that participants in Memory Bridge-hosted learning experiences are expected to adopt.

In so many different ways, people who have been in intimate company with a person with dementia have said to me, or to one of the groups of learners of which I have been a member: 'I could feel a connection.' Or: 'There was a connection there. I could feel it.' In the instances I have in mind, the person with dementia was believed to be beyond communication. Often, they were described as nonverbal. In none of these instances could the person with dementia speak 'normally'. What makes these testimonies so moving to me is experiencing the way they are shared. You can feel a spirit in the way the experiences themselves are communicated. It is as if the person with dementia is seeking to connect, through the person sharing the story, with other people too. It is as if the person with dementia is teaching us how little we actually understand about what the limits of communication are. It is as if the very word 'nonverbal' speaks to how little we are able to verbalise what can happen between two or more people when they come together with no desire other than to be in each other's company lovingly. It is as if – and I say this gently and speaking principally of myself – we really ought to be sensitive to how precious little we actually understand about what it means 'to have dementia'.

I guess you can see what I mean when I say that I am never sure how to answer people when they ask me how one bridges people to people with dementia. I suppose one actually doesn't. It apparently takes two at least: a person with dementia and a person without dementia. And I'm comfortable going on record as saying it takes three: a person with dementia, a person

> *without dementia, and a spirit – holy or otherwise – that moves between them. Memory Bridge's work bridging students and elders with dementia brought us into sustained contact with thousands of people living with dementia in many ethnic, social, and economic demographics, residing in both public supported and private pay residential communities.*
>
> *We soon realised that the most common denominator of people with dementia, irrespective of their cultural and economic background, was emotional isolation. We also learned that young people delighted in befriending people with dementia. The relationships offered the teens an opportunity to shed their everyday school personae and find a new sense of purpose in caring for those who are vulnerable. Both lessons – the isolation of elders and the enthusiasm of young people – decisively influenced Memory Bridge's growth. An urgent human need had been disclosed. We would invite, educate, and enable a kind of communication that is intrinsically healing and for which there is no medicinal or technological shortcut.*[7]

However, it should not be forgotten that as well as these positive experiences there can also be negative connotations to relationships. Without understanding that dementia is an interpersonal as well as a medical condition, we will not realise we can influence dementia's development through the quality of our caring. Some have suggested that any loss of self in a person living with dementia is the fault of those with whom they have relationships. Tom Kitwood argues that dementia is a condition which responds both to how we regard it and the person labelled with it, and the prevalent negative attitudes need to be challenged. He suggests that many supporting those living with dementia may be shocked to realise they have a huge part to play in creating the negative atmosphere many living with dementia have to endure. These include:

- *Treachery* – deceiving the person to get them to do what you want.
- *Disempowerment* – not allowing a person to carry out a task they are capable of doing.

- *Infantilisation* – treating an adult as if they were a child.
- *Ignoring* – speaking of a person in their presence as if they were not there.
- *Outpacing* – moving or speaking at a pace beyond the person's capability.[8]

Kitwood suggests that even good relationships can have drawbacks, such as 'letting ourselves be dependent on the goodwill of others and obligations to them'. This applies more to those living with dementia than most. Nevertheless, relationships are almost synonymous with meaning for people living with dementia. Experiences of many indicate that in rare moments of lucidity, the person is far more aware than previously thought. Indeed, it could be suggested that often the person isolated in their own world emerges when surrounded by continuous, loving, and faithful relationships, and that most people living with dementia retain some level of capacity which provide windows for connection and relationship.

'I don't visit her anymore, as she doesn't recognise me now, so there's no point', is a common misconception that presupposes the person has such poor quality of life that relationships have now become meaningless. However, Wendy Mitchell, another writer who lived with dementia, challenges this assumption, echoing the ideas explored earlier. 'Even though you may forget that your friends or family visited recently, what stays with you are the feelings of love, happiness and comfort when they were near. So even if they don't appear to remember, please don't ever stop visiting them.'[9] This thought is beautifully illustrated by the following story:

An older man arrived for an early morning appointment with his GP. He said he needed to be quick as he had another appointment at 9.00 am. The doctor asked if it was another medical appointment, as he was in such a hurry. He replied he needed to get to the nursing home to have breakfast with his wife. The doctor asked after her health, and he explained she was living with Alzheimer's disease. The doctor asked if she would

> *be upset if he was a bit late, and he replied she no longer knew who he was and hadn't recognised him in five years now. The doctor was surprised, and said, 'And you still go every morning, even though she doesn't know who you are?' He smiled, patted the doctor's hand and said, 'She may not know me, but I still know who she is.'*[10]

People living with dementia are still sensitive to honesty and kindness. Carl Rogers, the person-centred psychotherapist, identified three attitudes of a good carer: communicating empathy (being willing to enter their reality); authenticity (honesty about oneself); and warm, unconditional liking for them. These attitudes signify to the person living with dementia: 'It's okay; it's okay to be you; it's okay for us to be together.'

It can further be argued that entering another person's reality means accepting whatever situation they feel they are in, connecting with their emotions and being sensitive to whatever frame of reference they may use to make sense of their situation. 'Even those who appear inert can benefit from the simple, calm and holding presence of another human being who is prepared to be alongside them for a while in the "land of forgetfulness".'[11]

The decline in so many care-home residents during the Covid lockdown is a poignant reminder of just how essential relationships are for their good mental health. Simply expressing love to someone living with dementia is one of the best ways to make and keep contact. Regardless of the stage of the condition they are at, love shows them you accept them for who they are. The first step is to discard old expectations and learn to see the person in a new way. Perhaps the simplest summary is to suggest that in building relationships in a new way with those living with dementia, we should stop putting them in a separate world and realise we are integrally related with them.

For supporters or carers, Jennifer Bute suggested to me three principles we can put into action to improve our relationships with those living with dementia: remember there is always a reason why a person is behaving in a particular way; when facts are forgotten, feelings remain; and familiar patterns of behaviour continue.

Before being commissioned as an Anna Chaplain, I was a volunteer visitor to the home for several years. In those early days, as I tried to build relationships, I realised that many of the residents were losing their cognitive abilities but I was unsure how to respond. If they were 'living in the past', I wrongly assumed I should encourage them to 'return to the present'. When a lady was sitting in outdoor clothing and saying she was waiting to be collected to 'go home soon', I mistakenly thought I should explain this was her home now and no one was coming to collect her. If they were distressed because they were going to be 'late for school', I thought it seemed more honest to explain they were grown up now and no longer a school child.

But once I was commissioned as an Anna Chaplain, I attended workshops on relating to people living with dementia, and I received a copy of the *Anna Chaplaincy Handbook*, and learnt so much about how I should respond to those living with dementia by 'living in their world'. I found the following extracts particularly helpful in building relationships:

- Show interest and respect by maintaining eye contact and relaxed body language.
- Be calm, patient, and don't interrupt.
- Read facial expressions and gestures, for they are likely to reveal more than the person's words.
- Gestures may replace forgotten words.
- Enter their world with them. Whatever they are expressing is actually where they are in time.
- Offer comfort and reassurance, especially when a person is having difficulty expressing themselves.
- Validate their experience. For example, a response to a person saying they are angry about an injustice might be: 'I would be angry if that happened to me'. It shows that you have listened.

- Offer a best guess if you don't understand what is said and they are becoming agitated. Try again if they say 'no' to a guess.
- Avoid correcting them.
- If you know their personal history, use it for reminiscence.
- Do things to initiate fond memories such as humming a favourite song or talking about a favourite hobby or pet. Offer a familiar photo or object to prompt a story.
- Smells, taste, and touch are also strong memory triggers.
- The connection you make with them is not only a bright spot of meaning in their day, it is also a model to motivate others to be creative in their connections with them as well.[12]

Harvard University runs a course on managing happiness, and it highlights positive relationships as a key ingredient, as one news article summarised:

> *An 85-year Harvard study discovered that the most important thing that brings us happiness in life is positive relationships, and your friendships are a huge component. Maintaining long-term friendships that are stable is one of the seven practices of people who live to be happy and healthy, the study found. Yet, each of our friendships can look different, and it turns out that in fact they shouldn't all look the same. The renowned Greek philosopher Aristotle narrowed down three types of friendships. Arthur Brooks, a Harvard professor who teaches a course about how to manage happiness, believes we need all three types of friendship to truly feel happy in life.*[13]

This study was researched for healthy people, but could be even more relevant for those living with dementia. The article goes on to list the three types of friendship:

- *Utility friendships.* These are with people 'with whom you work or with whom you do business. These relationships tend to be transactional in nature.' For someone living with dementia, these could be the visiting GP, the district nurse, the chiropodist, or perhaps the cleaner.

- *Pleasurable friendships.* This type of relationship is based on each person drawing pleasure from the other. 'If a person finds their friend funny, interesting, and a source of enjoyment, it is likely to be a friendship of pleasure.' For someone living with dementia, this could be a long-standing friendship that predates their dementia or a favourite carer. It is wrong to assume that such friendships are one-sided, with the one living with dementia simply receiving from the other. I used to love visiting a resident in the local dementia care home. She always made me laugh, and I looked forward to visiting her, even though she was very confused and had very little memory recall. I visited her on the day before she died. Her last words to me were, 'Oh, I do love you, Wendy – you never mind that I am completely barmy!' A pleasurable friendship indeed (though 'barmy' is not a word I would use)!

- *'Perfect' friendships.* 'By Aristotle's standards, perfect friendships are those between people who have a mutual love for something [and are] focused on improving the circumstance of the other person.' For someone living with dementia, this could be the love they discover from their life-partner who supports and knows them, even if they are advanced on their dementia journey, or perhaps their pastor, Anna Chaplain, or spiritual carer. Such perfect friendships illustrate that the loving relationship is not one-sided – the love is shared. Robin Thomson gives an example that illustrates the importance of love for the person living with dementia. In his book, he describes how despite the discouragement and relentless pressure he experienced as his wife's dementia progressed, even more remarkable was 'my growing awareness of her constant affection and love, despite the decline in her mental ability'.[14]

In looking at relationships, there may not be great differences between the approaches of Christian and non-Christian supporters of those living with dementia, but there might be significant differences in why they follow their approach and the resources they use to do it well. Christians have unique resources, including the wisdom and love of God that comes from the indwelling of the Holy Spirit, the ability to pray for God's comfort and hope, and a church body willing to join in and help.

There is a wonderful vision in the book of Zechariah:

> *'Once again men and women of ripe old age will sit in the streets of Jerusalem, each of them with cane in hand because of their age. The city streets will be filled with boys and girls playing there.'*
>
> ZECHARIAH 8:4–5

This is a picture of a community of relationships, where people share together, and where those marginalised by dementia are at the centre of society, instead of ignored on the edge. This is the community that is illustrated by the apostle Paul in 1 Corinthians 12:12–31, where 'the parts that we think are less honourable we treat with special honour' (v. 23). It is my prayer that one day our society will embrace these values, and those living with dementia will no longer be the marginalised and forgotten, but be treated with the justice they deserve as a central, valued, and beloved part of the community.

And here is a final illustration of what a real relationship with someone living with dementia can be like. A four-year-old girl, Lisa, was visiting her grandparents, and her grandmother was living with advanced dementia. Lisa asked her grandfather if he would go away, because she wanted to be on her own with her granny. He retreated, and from a distance he watched their 'private time' unfold. Lisa first pranced in front of her granny, showing off her hair-bow, then softly took her granny's face in her little hands, and they made eye-to-eye contact, and finally she crawled on to her granny's lap and her granny glowed and smiled. Later in the day, the grandfather asked Lisa what she had been doing and talking about with her granny. Lisa looked completely perplexed and baffled. 'Grandpa,' she said, 'I wasn't doing anything, I wasn't talking about anything; I was just loving her.'[15]

6

Dementia and the arts, creation, and creativity

The great grace of God can be tasted in one small moment.
Henri Nouwen

Living in the present moment

If there is one thing that could be considered a gift of dementia, it is the capacity to find pleasure in the present moment. Perhaps someone living with dementia is actually experiencing what so many of us crave when we turn to mindfulness or meditation to practise the presence of God in the here and now?

In Exodus 3:14 God says to Moses, 'I AM WHO I AM'. The use of the present tense indicates that, from eternity past to eternity present, God is ever-present. Perhaps a simpler way of putting this is to say that God values the present. Those living with dementia also do this, especially as their condition progresses. They no longer worry about the future and become less and less conscious of the past. They may gradually become less interested in news of the world outside and will only care about how they feel in the here and now; they are not concerned about their loss of memory and other capacities. To respect their dignity, those around them must learn to enjoy the present moment with them. At times, being touched and held may be all they want. A supporter was talking about her friend living with dementia:

> *She is great! She used to plan a year in advance, but now she simply thinks of what's happening now, grateful for the present and that she's alive. And in a sense, that's how we all need to live, holding on to what we have now, because that's the only thing we truly know about.*[1]

Christine Bryden often writes about the importance of recognising that those living with dementia live in the present moment. She believes that many well people seek earnestly for a sense of the present time, the sense of 'now', of how to live each moment and treasure it as if it were the only experience to look at and wonder at. But she stresses that this is actually the experience of dementia – living life in the present without a past or a future. She says:

> *I continue to be me and see the world through my eyes in the present moment. I am who I am now and meaning is what I can find in this present moment. Even those living with later and last stages of dementia can continue to find meaningful narratives in the present moment. The fact that those of us living with dementia live in the present with a depth of spirit and some tangled emotions, rather than cognition, means others can connect with us at a deep level through touch, eye contact and smiles.*[2]

Being content in the present moment is beautifully illustrated by the experience of one Anna Chaplain. She had been visiting an older man who was really advanced in his dementia. She watched as his wife gently put his slippers on for him, and then asked him, 'When were you at your happiest, John?' He simply smiled at her and said, 'Now.'

The arts and creativity

Perhaps because of 'living in the moment', things come up fresh for those living with dementia and a sense of wonder is easier to come by. They have moved from intellect to emotion, so the emphasis on feeling over reasoning in the arts may make creativity especially appealing for someone living in the present whose cognition is declining. The arts are also about communication, and many don't involve words, but they do involve activity, doing something and being involved in the present moment, which provides an outlet for those for whom the verbal can cause problems.

One such lady reflects on the way dementia has freed her up for new experiences, while recognising that creativity may fulfil a new need she has developed:

> *I'm not saying that dementia is not serious. But I'm going to say that it's a licence in a way, a licence to be free, to be me. I think when I was diagnosed I was given permission to be more relaxed into this person and accept her. I wanted to find out if I was artistic. Creativity's an aspect I want to explore. It's a bit like waiting on Christmas. You know it's coming, but as a child you don't exactly know when. It's a nice feeling.*[3]

It is fascinating that artistic aptitudes in people living with dementia seem to come largely from this ability to be 'present in the moment'. Art of all sorts, whether art appreciation or creativity, enables people living with dementia and those without it to focus together on something outside themselves, rather than each other. John Zeisel explains that all these art skills link together separate brain locations in which memories and skills lie. The brain systems that are affected in this way are called 'distributed'. As the brain is affected in Alzheimer's disease and particular locations and abilities are damaged, the fact that art touches so many areas of the brain masks single-location deficits.[4] The more someone is in touch with their feelings, the more they can appreciate art. Because people living with dementia tend to express what they think and feel in that moment, they can be natural artists and natural audiences for artistic expression.

The artist Makoto Fujimura has written about the power of making something rather than being taught about it to experience God. While he was writing for people in general, his theories are particularly applicable to those living with dementia. He writes:

> *We don't need the process of taking in data to experience God – we can really experience him through the creative processes of painting, music, singing and poetry. Every time we create something we are experiencing the Holy Spirit.*

He takes this thought even further by suggesting that unless we are making something we cannot really experience the depth of God's grace permeating our lives: 'God is THE creator, and He will never be fully known simply by taking in information. It is the act of making/creating that can lead us to know THE creator personally.'[5] This is such a hopeful vision for those whose cognition is declining, but who can still enjoy making music, singing, painting, and poetry. Creativity enables people to continue to communicate without words.

Visiting art galleries or museums and attending poetry readings or concerts can provide meaning in what to many is experienced as an ever-increasingly meaningless life. Art connects people to their culture and their community. When art is a profound part of the everyday life for people living with dementia, it offers a vibrant and extraordinary dimension. Oliver Sacks, the neurologist, commented on the process of taking groups of people living with dementia to look at pictures in a gallery:

> *Certainly, it's not just a visual experience – it's an emotional one. In an informal way I have often seen patients with advanced dementia recognise and respond vividly to paintings at a time when they are scarcely responsive to words and disoriented out of it. I think that recognition of visual art can be very deep.*

He further suggests that people whose cognition is declining are still able to understand visual art by:

- *Perceiving and describing* – talking about what they see in the artwork.
- *Telling a story* – narrating the story they see in the picture.
- *Linking it to their own lives* – describing personal memories.
- *Identifying the emotion* – naming and expressing the emotions in the artwork.
- *Identifying objects* – seeing, naming, and describing objects in the artwork.
- *Making critical judgements* – commenting on moral issues raised in risqué artwork.[6]

Music

About a decade ago, researchers discovered that when people listened to music, multiple areas of the brain were involved in processing it. These included the limbic (which processes emotions and memory), cognitive (involved with perception, learning, and reaction), and motor areas (responsible for voluntary movement). This challenged preconceptions that music was processed more narrowly in the brain, and it helped explain why it has such a unique neurological impact.

Not only that, but research has also shown that music might help regenerate the brain and its connections. Many causes of dementia centre around cell death in the brain, raising the possibility that music could help people living with dementia by mending or strengthening damaged neural connections and cells. A small study conducted by the Cambridge Institute for Music Therapy Research found that when people living with dementia repeatedly listened to their favourite music, their heart rate and movements changed in direct response. This showed that people's physical responses were affected by musical features like rhythm and arrangement. Their heart rate also changed when they sang along to music or when they began reminiscing about old memories or stories while listening to a song or thinking about the music. These changes are important because they show how music affects movement, emotions, and memory recall.

Studies have also shown that during and after listening to music, people living with dementia experienced less agitation, aggression, and anxiety, and their general mood was improved. They even needed less medication when they had regular music sessions.[7]

Carey Smith Henderson writes:

> *I've always loved music very deeply and I find this a solace. I've whiled away many hours listening to music and feel that I'm still doing something I love. I can't make music any more, but I can certainly use it for my own intentions – which are just to be beautiful.*[8]

Music helps most people living with dementia come to life – sometimes people think this is sweet, but it is more than that. People don't lose their memories when they have dementia, it is just that they can't access them. Music bridges that gap – it fills people with emotion and acts as a bridge to access memories and experiences. Those who have become quiet and withdrawn can become quite animated when they listen to music. This is not just cute – they are experiencing what has become unavailable to them through the neural pathways that have been damaged by the effects of the dementia. The after-effects can linger long after the songs or music have ended.

Community worship with the inclusion of singing traditional and contemporary hymns are wonderful ways to stimulate and promote brain health, as well as nurture the spiritual needs of a church member living with dementia. The 'Singing for the Brain' programme of the Alzheimer's Society may seem simply like a sing-along, but it is much more than that. The programme provides carers and people living with dementia a social life with one another. The songs, limericks, breathing exercises, and laughter provide carer/person couples something to focus on other than the person's condition. Each song in a 'Singing for the Brain' session is focused on eliciting a particular emotion and movement.[9]

If you create a singing event in your care home, you may get a surprise gift of a musical memory. My own most poignant experiences have often been in seeing how even those most lost to their dementia become aroused and able to join in singing the songs of their childhood, showing that people living with dementia can still grow in faith and experience.

I was recently leading a short service in our dementia care home, using some old, well-known hymns that many of them knew. When we had finished singing 'Jesus loves me', one lady, who was usually morose and fairly silent, got to her feet and walked to the centre of the room. She said, 'I used to be a singer, you know', and proceeded to sing 'Little boy kneels at the foot of the bed' from 'Christopher Robin'. She was absolutely word- and pitch-perfect and sang the entire song without any help or prompting! After we all applauded her, she returned to her chair, where she sat beaming and responsive for ages, and of course it was a wonderful topic for conversations with her for many visits afterwards.

Another example also happened after we had been singing. One lady was still verbal, but obviously unhappy and increasingly withdrawn. As we sang, I noticed that she was 'playing' the notes with her fingers on her knees. When we had finished singing our songs she beckoned me over, and told me she had been a piano teacher and how much she missed her pupils. One of the support staff overheard, and told her he had always wanted to learn the piano and would she like to teach him? So, for the next few weeks whenever he had a break they would sit at the piano together, and she taught him some simple tunes. The next month when we had a service, he was able to play a basic hymn tune, and she sat beaming proudly at him, completely transported back to her earlier life.

On another occasion I noticed one lady who rarely spoke (and who I had assumed was now non-verbal) was joining in a familiar hymn.

When I said, 'You knew all the words of that song didn't you, Rose?' she replied happily, 'Yes, it's all about God, you know.'

Another experience comes from a pastor writing about finding Christ in dementia:

> *I vividly recall one chapel service in which a woman with dementia sat in a wheelchair. She was curled in on herself, and said nothing, but a few quiet babbled sounds. Yet when the first notes of the hymn 'All hail the power of Jesus' name' were played, she uncurled, looked up, smiled, and then sang every word of every verse from memory. Sceptics may account for this by saying the mind can randomly misfire, but it appears to happen too often with Christian songs and liturgy to be coincidence.*[10]

A similar illustration is of a former pastor who is living with quite advanced dementia. He had lost the ability to speak, and one day his daughter read him some scripture verses, and then sang quietly, 'Jesus loves me, this I know'. She heard him say 'Again,' so, surprised, she sang it again, and once more he said 'Again.' This time he began to sing it with her, hesitantly at first and then more confidently. It was not a mindless repetition, but an act of worship. His regular carer came into the room and stood still, eyes wide with astonishment.[11]

The perception of music and the emotions it can stir is not solely dependent on memory, and dementia is no barrier to emotional depth. Someone living with dementia can find listening to music a consoling experience, and most certainly, music is one of the most important and sometimes dramatic ways of connecting with someone living with dementia.

Poetry

Poetry is another art form that turns on parts of the brain that mere words do not. The reading and writing of poetry cut across the brain's disfunctions, enabling people living with dementia to participate fully. Writing a poem about how you or a loved one has been affected by dementia can offer relief for both writer and reader. For those who struggle to explain their feelings, it can also provide a powerful insight into what dementia means for those living with it every day.

The following poem was written by someone who had been recently diagnosed with dementia:

Sometimes I picture myself
like a candle.
I used to be a candle about eight feet tall –
Burning bright.
Now, every day I lose a little bit of me.
Someday the candle will be
very small
But the flame will be
just as bright.[12]

Susanna Howard employs the technique of using words uttered by people living with severe dementia to create pieces and word books for them. She is the artistic director of Living Words, 'an arts charity designed to foster creative communication with people who have dementia', which she founded in 2007. Through Living Words, artists and writers have developed an approach called 'Listen Out Loud': 'Over several weeks, Living Words members meet with people living with dementia one-on-one, listening to their feelings and reflecting their words to help them feel heard and valued.'[13] Working with individuals to edit in a non-intellectual way, a person's words become pieces with their own Living Words booklet, for them to keep and carers read with them to support communication.[14]

After creating such a piece with one lady, Howard recalls that the lady, Angela, took her hand and said: 'Now you know two worlds, the one outside and the one inside in me, and you must go and tell all the people.' And 'telling the people' is what Living Words does! Living Words' communication workshops are for both those living with dementia and their caregivers, to help discover the needs of those living with dementia and how they express themselves. Howard writes that she finds it 'very sad when people say the essence of a person goes when they have dementia... I believe the person you loved is still there, operating from their essential self, free of the ego that created the person you knew.'[15]

The following poignantly expresses an example of her work. Ellen has advanced dementia, and verbal communication can be a struggle for her. Howard sits with her, quietly waiting. Finally, a single word emerges from Ellen's lips: 'Human', she says. Howard jots this on her notepad and resumes waiting. Over a long time, with help from Howard, Ellen's utterances slowly take on a totally new form – a poem:

King or Queen

It's called 'Patient Condition'
You must not just say
'Good morning,' 'Goodbye'
It minimizes the relationship
Try and appraise, interest
Tenderness, consciousness, confidence
The fact that you are sharing with them
Uplift the feeling
'Feel better already,'
Make us feel human
Not just a dummy.
Pretend you have all the time
In the world
We feel like King or Queen.[16]

A similar method is used by John Killick. Over many weeks he forges a relationship with an individual before composing a poem. He looks for the emotional thread when crafting these poems and then reads it to them and, if possible, their relatives. He has a golden rule: he never adds anything to their words, only takes some away.

Reactions vary. Some reject them as worthless, but at the other extreme he is told, 'Publish it!' His second golden rule is to abide by the person's decision, or sometimes the relatives step in and make the decision on the person's behalf. The majority of people appear to value the process tremendously. It is confirmation for them that their words are being taken seriously and a confirmation for readers that it is worth communicating with people living with dementia.[17]

The following poem was created in this way:

When I had the stroke
The feeling crept up my body like lightness
Like I was a cloud high up
Like I was going to float away
And I was getting lighter and lighter all the time.
Since then
I haven't had a fear of dying
Because I know that's what it will be like
Don't be afraid of it
Because the feeling was wonderful.[18]

John Zeisel writes of an Alzheimer's poetry project, which involves helping everyone in the room to participate. In one instance they were all asked to say a line in answer to the question, 'What is the most beautiful thing you ever saw?' Everyone participated, and the 'most beautiful' poem was greeted with joy and enthusiasm by all of them.[19]

Reading poetry to someone living with dementia can also be rewarding. Traditional poems that people find engaging have certain characteristics that work: they have strong images; they use bold images of nature; they are possibly well-known from childhood; they have short stanzas; or they may be short overall. Just a few that reflect these characteristics are:

- 'Sonnet 18: Shall I compare thee to a summer's day?', William Shakespeare, 1609
- 'The Tyger', William Blake, 1794
- 'I wandered lonely as a cloud', William Wordsworth, 1807
- 'How do I love thee?' (sonnet 43), Elizabeth Barrett Browning, 1850
- 'The arrow and the song', Henry Wadsworth Longfellow, 1845
- 'The owl and the pussy-cat', Edward Lear, 1871
- 'The road not taken', Robert Frost, 1916
- 'Sea-Fever', John Masefield, 1902
- 'The house with nobody in it', Joyce Kilmer, 1914
- Any poems at all by Pam Ayres!

Creative therapy

Almost any creative activity can be a bridge, or sometimes stepping stones, to find someone's inner core. There are many activities that can bring meaning: looking at photos, previously loved hobbies such as stamp collecting or gardening, simple word and number games, soft ball games, and puppets.

When I was a counsellor, I often used the creative therapy of painting, sand trays, dolls, and puppets. I discovered that the power of creativity to connect people with their unconscious memories and emotions was much faster than through conversation alone. So, in my work as an Anna Chaplain, I decided to try using a life-like therapy doll to connect with the residents in the care home. As I walked into the room cradling the doll, several immediately started smiling. Even the most withdrawn became quite engaged when I asked for suggestions for a name for her (the final decision was 'Olivia'), and almost everyone seemed pleased and put their arms out when asked if they would like to hold her. While most ladies would cradle and talk lovingly to Olivia, one used to scold her, and wag her finger at her – perhaps remembering some naughty child of her own! One lady, who initially was very hostile to the idea of cuddling a doll, became quite animated once she actually had her in her arms, and started a loud conversation about the benefits of breastfeeding.

A therapy doll doesn't have to be just for the ladies. As I passed the doll around the room, the only gentleman present put his hands out to hold her. He usually used very little eye contact and was taciturn with others, despite often talking loudly to himself. As he took the doll, I was surprised to see him turn her over, and look at the label on the back of her neck. His face broke into a large grin, and he looked directly at me as he said, 'I used to own a toy shop, and we sold this brand of doll!' This led to a really meaningful conversation with him about his career in the toy industry. Subsequently, he was much more engaged with me when I led worship, which he had previously ignored.

However, be aware that some relatives may initially think handling dolls is making their loved one too childlike or patronised. But in my own experience dolls bring nothing but pleasure and even joy. Giving them a doll to cuddle seems to bridge the communication gap, while providing the person with a rare opportunity to become a nurturer, and give instead of always receiving. And of course, for those who have been mothers, it triggers some wonderful maternal memories of babies they might have forgotten. Perhaps I should also add that in all the research I have done into this subject, I have found no mention of the possible benefits to the helper. In my early days I found it daunting to visit some of the more challenging residents, and the doll was both a comfort and a distraction, helping me relax and reducing any tension in the room.

Another creative activity the residents in my care home always enjoyed was decorating small mirrors with stick-on flowers and letters, which they could then keep on their bedside tables, or give to a relative as a gift. On one occasion during a Messy Vintage Church[20] session we had been helping the residents decorate mirrors with the words 'God loves me'. On gently asking one usually silent resident, 'Do you realise how much God loves you, Jane?', she immediately responded with a radiant smile, 'Oh yes, and I love him right back every day!' When I visited her the next week, she had completely forgotten about the mirror, but when I prayed with her she smiled at me and said, 'I love God always in my heart.' She then told me a long and animated story about going on a church picnic with her parents when she was a little girl!

Another lady, Monica, had been withdrawn and reclusive in her room, until she received a 'kindness card' from a child in our church. This simple gesture encouraged her to start to come out and join in with our activities. When she was decorating her mirror, she asked if she could choose any words of her own, and completely unaided she wrote, 'Monica prays'. From then on she joined in the worship with a smile on her face.

One Easter when I visited our local dementia care home, I took every resident a small wooden holding cross. We sang some worship songs, and then I suggested they hold their crosses while we prayed to remind them how much God loves them and that he is listening to their prayers. Having something tangible to hold seemed to be a real trigger for even those living with advanced dementia who would normally be unresponsive. They looked at their crosses, joined in the words of the Lord's Prayer, and two ladies had tears running down their cheeks as they prayed.

All the creative experiences mentioned in this chapter are successful when they hold on to the fundamental principle that as access to memory wanes in dementia, creativity can remain vibrant and alive. As Dorothy Sayers wrote: 'The characteristic common to God and to man is apparently the desire and the ability to make things.'[21]

Creation

Finally, for those who are losing their cognitive abilities, simply enjoying creation can be a springboard for experiencing God. In her book, *God's Not Forgotten Me*, 'Tricia Williams quotes Matthew, living with dementia. Matthew, who had limited mobility, spent much of his time looking out of the window at his garden. 'Tricia asked if his dementia was making him feel differently about God. After a long pause, he answered: 'Yes, I think so. Because I look out and see the birds of the air... and in the book of Genesis God created the sea and birds that sweep over the sea.' Matthew's words 'the birds of the air' bring to mind the words of Jesus in Matthew 6:26, which speak of not being worried and trusting instead in God's care. Matthew seems to be thinking about God's role in creation and seemed to relish this with his poetic words, 'sweep over'. His words seemed to suggest the evidence he was seeing in creation of God's power and care.[22]

Spending time in nature, smelling the roses, watching the waves on the sea, looking at the stars, listening to music, taking part in creative activities – these can all be used to bring God's love to someone and reconnect them to their story. When I was talking with Jennifer Bute, she said she found one of the most evocative ways of feeling God's presence is in the sound of water, whether in the noise of crashing waves or the gentler babbling sounds of a stream or a garden water feature, as they remind her of the words of Jesus – 'Whoever believes in me... rivers of living water will flow from within them' (John 7:38). Indeed, emotional healing and wholeness can be provided in such non-verbal ways, and often addresses needs far more effectively than any amount of cognitive understanding.

Robert Davis writes movingly of how his dementia seems to be cutting him off from all his usual ways of meeting God – church services, Bible class, reading – and asks: 'How did people meet God before there were books?' Then he remembers the scripture: 'The heavens declare the glory of God; the skies proclaim the work of his hands... their voice goes out into all the earth, their words to the ends of the world' (Psalm 19:1, 4). He writes:

> *So now I am finding joy in God's creation. It speaks to me of my heavenly Father who cares for the birds of the air and the flowers of the field. Believe it or not, I am comforted even by watching televised nature shows. As I see the intricately tuned balance of nature with a place for each creature great and small, I am reassured that God still knows my name even if I can't hear him in the ways I once did.*[23]

All these examples of creative ways to share God's love and find a bridge into someone's story are a touching reminder of needs to be met, which include comfort, inclusion, and occupation. Christine Bryden echoes this thought when she writes that she needs others to support her spiritually, by relating not to her mind but to her soul within her, by singing alongside her, offering appropriate touch, praying with her, and reassuring her of their presence and through them of Christ's presence.

7

Living with dementia and still communicating with God

Are your wonders known in the darkness, or your saving help in the land of forgetfulness?
PSALM 88:12 (NRSV)

Chapter 1 explored the feelings expressed by some who are actually living with dementia themselves. In this chapter, we share the experiences of Anna Chaplains and others who care for the spiritual well-being of those living with dementia. It is significant that all these Christian supporters are respecting the inherent dignity of those with dementia, and in so doing they are honouring God. Dunlop suggests that this happens because 'the dignity of everyone, including those with dementia, is rooted in nothing less than the fact that they were made in the image of God.'[1]

The experiences explored so far have related mainly to people in the early or mid-stages of their dementia journey. This chapter is about those who are living through the advanced stages of the condition. Often non-verbal, and increasingly living in 'the land of forgetfulness', it could easily be assumed that they are now unaware of their relationship with God. However, these wonderful, hope-filled testimonies illustrate that no one is ever beyond the reach of God's loving touch.

Some anecdotes are brief, others are longer. The names of contributors have been omitted, and where names of those being described are used, they have been changed to preserve their anonymity. I am so grateful for all the contributions I have received.

From a granddaughter

My grandmother lived with dementia for over 20 years, while being cared for by us, her family. Keeping her connected with all that was important to her in her faith and Christian life was a key part to caring for her.

We got her to church every week, in the wheelchair, and although she looked as though she was asleep at times, her foot-tapping during hymns showed she was aware of what was going on. It was a time of peace and comfort.

She often had hymns playing in her room.

Bedtime was another key time. We used to pray with her every evening as we laid her down to sleep. I think she had a blood rush to the brain as she was often very lucid at this point! She finished the ends of prayers and sang with us and showed deep appreciation for these times.

On one occasion, before she lost the ability to speak completely, she described a beautiful place she could see, while lying in bed with her eyes shut, after one of these times of prayer and praise. She had a wonderful look of peace on her face.

We sang simple choruses to her, like 'Jesus loves me this I know' and 'Wide, wide as the ocean'. These truths were as important for us to hear and repeat as for her. One night I sang the latter about 40 times before she finally fell asleep!

When visiting a lady with dementia in a care home, who knew her Bible well, reading psalms to her used to settle her confusion and calm her obsessive questions or frustrations.

I can't think of a better thing to do with someone living with dementia than hold their hand and speak or sing key Bible truths!

From a son

My father, Peter, had advanced dementia and his particular area of difficulty was his memory – he simply lived in the present moment.

My mother, Margaret, played his favourite sermons and in that moment his relationship with God was 100% focused and totally fulfilled. Margaret then revisited these sermons after a few days as he had forgotten, but could then enjoy them all over again.

In the same way, Peter enjoyed his favourite worship music – in the present moment – and prayer.

Peter's Christian belief was not impacted by his condition. He trusted the loving guidance and care of his wife Margaret and appreciated her supply of God-focused moments through the day.

Peter needed a wheelchair in the last six months of his life. This made church attendance more difficult, but the church community helped get him there for special church events.

Margaret used a daily reading and prayer book specifically designed for those living with dementia and their supporters: Worshipping with Dementia *by Louise Morse.*

From an Anna Chaplaincy lead chaplain

I was sitting with a dying, non-verbal patient. He was completely lost and disengaged. But as soon as I said I was going to pray for him, he made direct eye contact with me and kept holding my gaze throughout the prayers.

There was another wheelchair-bound, non-responsive patient – he was obviously listening as I read some parables. When we started singing 'Amazing Grace', he lifted up his arm and held firmly on to my hand until we finished singing the song.

During our Easter Messy Vintage service we were making Easter gardens with little pebbles to make a pathway. A usually non-responsive patient suddenly started picking up pebbles and completed the whole path by himself! He continued to be alert for several days afterwards, much to the amazement and delight of his wife and the caring staff.

From a spiritual supporter

Catherine was a much-loved member of our congregation, always positive and joyful and deeply committed to Jesus. As she turned 90, she began to show signs of forgetfulness, and her dementia became more evident over the next couple of years. She got increasingly confused about finances, she would say that nobody had visited her that day (although they had), and she constantly forgot most of our names. Timings became confused, eating became erratic.

Eventually a care home became the only option, though she was regularly collected in a car by a member of the congregation so she could still come to church services – which she loved despite seemingly dozing throughout. She clearly valued being there and the sense that people were greeting her, but two-way communication became a thing of the past, and often chats consisted of friendly disjointed sentences and comments – though she was always clear that Jesus loved her.

About a month before she died, I was with Catherine after a Sunday morning service, and I offered to pray for her. After doing so, to my great surprise, Catherine offered to pray for me – and what a prayer! Totally lucid, totally articulate, totally to the point! I was so incredibly humbled and blessed by the Spirit that was so deep within her that it was clearly more integral to her than any short-term memory loss.

From an author and champion of those living with dementia

The most important aspect of dementia care is spiritual support and input. Even when the condition has changed someone's behaviour to the point they seem to have 'gone', in fact the essence of them, the person, remains. I have many stories of people responding to spiritual input, from 'rementing' – gaining lucidity for a little while – to coming to faith. Even in the deepest dementia.

I see this with a dear friend who used to be my counselling supervisor. She has been married for 62 years, and her husband, a retired pastor and evangelist, is in the fourth year of Alzheimer's/vascular dementia. About 18 months ago he'd stopped speaking, so I took over a copy of a workbook I'd developed called Brain and Soul Boosting, *thinking it might help. And I still have her message on WhatsApp telling me how he looked at it, picked it up, and then led them through it! He is still talking, though not volubly or always coherently.*

From my observations and others' experience, it isn't that people with dementia adapt their communication with God. It's that he keeps his promise and never leaves or forsakes them. His Spirit communicates with their spirit. They can't hold on to him, but he holds on to them.

An example comes from the daughter of a former Baptist pastor now living with dementia in a care home. He stopped speaking for a few months. She and her husband still visited regularly, and on one visit he regained lucidity for a little while, and told them that in his silence God had been speaking to him. God gave him a verse that so blessed him he was able to accept his losses and find peace. It was Psalm 37:24 – 'Though he may stumble, he will not fall, for the Lord upholds him with his hand.'

From an Anna Chaplain

I lead an inclusive friendship group, with a special welcome to those living with dementia, as well as their supporters, family, and friends. A dear older lady living with dementia was a regular attendee and was limited in her ability to communicate and take part in activities. However, she responded to hugs and the touching of hands and face. Each week she would ask my name, and would respond by sharing a hug, and she said my hugs warmed her heart. One day, I asked her if she would like to go for a walk, and I took her into our church memorial garden. We sat on a bench under a tree, holding hands. She told me she could hear the birds singing, and then she said she could feel Jesus sitting with us, and she started to sing 'All things bright and beautiful' and we sang a few verses together.

From a widow

In his last months, despite Christopher finding it hard to express himself coherently, he would readily tell his testimony of how he became a Christian when he was 17, and how that led to his family becoming Christians.

He prayed regularly at his homegroup, which was on Zoom at the time during Covid. He remained able to sing and being part of the choir was the highlight of his week. He was still able to say Grace before meals if invited to do so.

When a friend read scripture with him in his final weeks he would join in with many of the words, and always say 'Amen'. In his final days he would greet his doctor (who was a Christian) with 'Hallelujah, Christ is Risen.' He knew his Saviour to the end.

From an Anna Chaplain

I'm an Anna Chaplain in a small rural parish. My ministry includes worship in our care homes for older people, three of which are specifically for those on the dementia pathway. So often, when telling them a Bible story I feel that I have probably lost most of them en route, even though I often tell it in my own words, keep it simple, and always remind them of how much they are all loved by God.

One day I was talking to them about Jesus' love for little children and explaining that what Jesus loves about children is their innocence, openness, and that they accept others without judging them, as many of us adults do. In the corner of the lounge was a lady who always sat in the same chair in the same place, quite still with her eyes closed, rocking back and forth in her chair. She never spoke or opened her eyes during any of my visits, but this time it was different. When I had finished my story she suddenly opened her eyes, looked straight at me and in a really loud voice said that she was one of Jesus' children and that he also loved her very much. Then she closed her eyes and started rocking once again. This lady, who was quite far down the dementia pathway had heard and understood what I said, and had remembered she was loved by God.

It was such a humbling reminder that we must never assume that someone with dementia automatically lacks the ability to hear and understand what we are saying. And I think that although they may not grasp everything, they do tune in to our gentle and caring tone of voice and words that are repeated to them, e.g. 'God loves us all so much.'

From the founder of a national organisation for older people

I had a lovely experience recently. I visit a lady with very advanced dementia in a care home. She is often in bed when I visit these days. My role is as a befriender, rather than chaplaincy. But a few weeks ago, her daughter messaged me to say that her mum might enjoy me reading the Bible to her. I knew she sometimes attended the church services at the care home, and the daughter knows that I am a Christian, but I didn't know anything else about her faith journey, and her Bible is an old English King James Version. I didn't know whether her faith was just a nominal part of her life. So, when I visited I asked her if she would like me to read the Bible to her, and she said, 'Yes, please!' I asked her if she had any favourite parts that she would like me to read and she said simply, 'Jesus.' I was so touched. This is a lady who doesn't know who I am from week to week, and sometimes when I visit her she might be convinced we are on a train or somewhere else. Yet she was immediate in her response that she wanted me to read to her about Jesus!

From a church pastoral assistant

For more than a decade, I have shared in ministry at our local residential care home. It is a privilege to have the opportunity to join in worship with those who are no longer able to attend church. We are always warmly received by staff and residents. Members of staff say that they appreciate the music from the service, as the sound permeates the house. I sense that our worship impacts the atmosphere. As a visiting team, we often feel greatly blessed ourselves – the residents minister to us too.

There was a dear Salvation Army lady. Joy always beamed from her face. She once preached a whole sermon with one sentence, using the following words: 'Whenever I feel down, I think about the Lord, and then I feel better.' That quote made its way into a sermon in church! She also spoke about seeing angels in the days before she died.

I remember another lady who was initially hostile. She spoke out once during the service saying, 'He wants me to submit to him, but I won't!' Weeks later there was a change. She was seen smiling and moving her arm in time with the music of the hymns.

Another lady, who was initially fully mobile, would always get up and go upstairs when we arrived for the service. Sometime later she would remain in the room, but would speak mockingly while the leader was speaking. She gradually softened with time. There was a very memorable occasion, when she responded in the affirmative when I asked her if she would like us to pray for her during a service of Holy Communion. Her face beamed as we prayed for her. I sensed that she was experiencing the presence of the Holy Spirit. At the time of writing, she is now frail, and not expected to be here on earth for much longer. She no longer speaks, but follows me with her eyes when I go into her room to pray with her.

She has no relatives. No one ever visits her. But I really sense that she has responded to Jesus and that in due course she will go to be with him.

Ministering to these dear people is important to me, because they are precious to God. Some may not have given much time to thinking about him during their busy lives, but if they are willing to give the Lord a place in their hearts towards the end of life's journey, he is as ready and as willing as ever to welcome them into his family.

From an Anna Chaplain

I want to share the power of gathering for a service of worship in the local care home. Those in the dementia unit love coming over and feel snubbed if there is nobody available to bring them across! There is joy in being together celebrating and singing the hymns that are remembered.

One lady that we visit loves talking to us (Anna Chaplains) when we visit. She tells us how she used to go to church and in her manner and her smile she shows how this played an important part in her life. She posed the question of what happens after death, what heaven is like, and what part of us goes to heaven. She's not worried – just curious. She has a very simple view that God/Jesus wouldn't tie himself up into getting trapped into cultural niceties, e.g. British people not talking about sex!

There is a gentleman in the dementia unit who says that he does not have faith, but he is still interested in whether he has any relatives still alive, and concentrates on his limited life on earth.

From the chaplain of the website 'Spiritual Eldercare'

This is why I love doing what I do. Every single time that I lead a Bible study or worship service for people living with Alzheimer's, I see miracles. These dear ones say things you would never expect someone with dementia to be able to say. They praise God with tears in their eyes. They come to life – even if just for a moment – with gratitude for how God is with them. They recall scriptures hidden in their hearts for decades. I can assure you that even when people seem 'gone' in the fog of dementia, God never stops reaching out to bring them joy and hope. Their spirits are very much alive, and God has not forgotten them. He is the good shepherd, bringing his lambs home. He is always, always active.

Once I was leading a scripture discussion on Romans 8:31–38 with a group of older people, most of whom have dementia. One woman was somewhat agitated, saying, 'Help me, help me,' and her caregiver almost took her away so as not to disturb the group. But I turned to her and started loudly reading, 'For I am convinced that neither death nor life, nor angels nor rulers, nor things present nor things to come, nor powers, nor height nor depth, nor anything else in all creation', and then paused. Without missing a beat, this woman raised her hand and finished the verse, saying clearly, 'Will be able to separate us from the love of God in Christ Jesus' (vv. 38–39, ESV). Another woman, who was new to the group that day, simply put her hand over her heart, closed her eyes, and said, 'Magnificent.'

Another time, studying Psalm 103, I asked: 'What does it mean that God "forgives all your iniquity" and "heals all your diseases" (v. 3)?' One woman piped up, 'God is a doctor!' And when we discussed 'forget not all his benefits' (v. 2), I asked, 'What benefits have you seen from God in your life?' People answered so quickly I had trouble writing them all down: 'Being born'; 'Family'; 'He heals all your diseases'; 'He's always there'; 'His faithfulness'; 'The luckiest I've ever been in when I found my wife'; 'Joy'. And one guy enthusiastically and wonderfully answered, 'I'm not done yet!'

From an Anna Chaplain

There is a wonderful lady in the care home I visit. She used to be a music teacher and choir mistress, and led the young people's group in our church for many years. Her faith meant everything to her. Her advancing dementia has meant she has gradually lost her communication skills, and she hardly speaks any more. But she has not forgotten how to sing, and spends most of her day singing the tunes of various worship songs, either in her own room or in the residents' lounge. If I sit and sing with her, the words come back to her as well. The staff and residents really appreciate her, and it is as if she still has the gift of being an evangelist. Her whole face lights up when anyone talks to her about Jesus.

From an ex-Anglican priest, now a care home chaplain

A person living with advanced dementia (from parish days) was very distressed and yelling at me using a wonderful array of vocabulary. I had been left on my own with a group as I celebrated the Eucharist with them. I had to make the decision what would be less disruptive – to go and find help to have the said resident moved or to plough on. Thankfully, I chose the latter and when I came to administer the sacrament it was as though the cloak of distress fell away as she raised her hands to receive this gift. She totally calmed, and my memory is that that in some way calmed the whole group towards receiving what is always a mystery. It was very powerful.

Some years ago, I read a book that quite inspired me: Eileen Shamy's A Guide to the Spiritual Dimension of Care for People with Alzheimer's Disease and Related Dementia *and it serves me well now. In this book Shamy recounts the story of a woman with dementia called May, who hadn't spoken for six months. The chaplain, knowing she wasn't a religious woman, gathered her family together and asked them to think what resources May had used to nourish her spirit. The family remembered that during a very dark period of the war – when she didn't hear from her husband for weeks, in the Blitz – her close friend's baby had died from a bomb. She used to go into the park alone and walked and walked under the trees, the oaks, the elms, beech, and sycamore trees. One daughter remembered her saying about that time that 'the trees gave me their strength'. The next fine day it was arranged for May to be wheeled to the park and the staff put her chair under a tree and withdrew. She seemed to relax, looked up at the tree, tears began to fall. Later she was taken home and when being put to bed she whispered, 'I tasted the sky. God held me up.' Within the week May had died.*

I constantly try to find the 'key' that might unlock the spirit of someone and so be able to nourish them during the end-of-life stage. This week, holding her hand, I sang to a Catholic lady 'Make me a channel of your peace', knowing that she used it when she prepared children for their first Communion. Having said very little up until then, she began joining in! Familiar hymns often unlock residents' voices – even if they barely speak, they often sing or certainly can become animated rocking to the rhythm. I have a resident who is French and when I played an Édith Piaf song that her sons had told me she used to like, she became really engaged. No longer really able to receive the sacrament, I feel music is sacramental to her and gives that sacramental nourishment.

From a website on faith in old age

I had the privilege of talking with committed Christians who are living with dementia. They spoke passionately about their continuing – even growing – faith and confidence in Christ… [One example:] 'God is always with me… and I know nothing can ever separate me from him… but now, even when my brain falls apart… it doesn't matter'… And questions about dementia making them feel distant from God brought assertions of the opposite – 'Closer,' [one lady] exclaimed… In dementia, my expressions of trust in Christ might be a simple 'Amen', a quiet humming of 'Jesus loves me, this I know', or a momentary smile expressing acknowledgment of him… God's grace trumps cognitive capacity.[2]

From the author of a book about living with dementia[3]

I remember visiting a nursing home with a group from our church to sing to the residents in their dining room. Before our concert we visited some of the residents who were confined to their beds. We asked if they would like us to sing for them, and as soon as we started to sing 'Amazing Grace' one of the ladies started to sing with us, and joined in every single word! I asked if I could pray with her before we left, and she said she would like that also. I began to pray, and she started to pray as well. She pleaded with her Lord to take her home, and how beautifully real and earnest her prayer was! She was so connected to him in spite of her confusion!

I was so overwhelmed with the realisation that although the mind may be confused, the spirit is still connected to God! He can still move our hearts, and he can still use us to bless others, whether we realise it or not. She most likely had no idea how God had used her to bless me that day!

From an Anna Chaplain

Since you asked for anecdotes about people living with dementia who are still aware of God, I have started looking on YouTube. There are several very poignant videos on this subject. One is of a lady sitting talking to her husband and her two sons. They ask her in turn, 'Do you know who I am?' And each time she says, 'No, I don't know you,' or, 'I think you visit me sometimes.' Then they ask her, 'Do you know who Jesus is?' And her face lights up, and she bangs her hand rhythmically on the table and says, 'Of course, I know Jesus. He is my Saviour, and he saved me, and he loves me, and I talk to him all the time.'

Another one is of a lady sitting talking with her carer, who asks her, 'Do you know what your address is?' And she says, 'No idea.' The carer says, 'Okay. Do you know what you had for lunch today?' And she says, 'Food, I suppose.' The carer replies, 'Okay. So, tell me, who is Linda?' And she says, 'I don't know any Linda.' So then the carer says, 'Okay. So what about Paul?' And she still looks mystified, and says, 'I don't know any Paul.' So finally, the carer asks her, 'So, who is Jesus?' And she immediately looks right at him and says, 'Jesus is my Saviour. He lives in my heart. And one day he has promised to take me home.'

From a son

My dad had been a lifelong atheist when he developed dementia. It became quite advanced and coherent conversation was no longer possible. I realised I could not discuss the gospel with him in the usual way, so I decided to read the Bible to him, but inserting his name into the narrative. When we got to John 3:16, and I started to read, 'God so loved Trevor', before I could continue to the next phrase, Dad said, 'I know, I know, "… that he gave his only Son for me." I know that.' He would then repeat that Jesus died for him, over and over. I am convinced he had accepted Christ and died a Christian.

From a nursing home carer

During Covid, no residents could attend church and no minister was allowed into the home. So, I offered to run 'services' for residents. One of the residents, Sarah, used to attend my church. Her decline from a quiet, very loving soul, doing a lot in the church, to someone with behavioural issues, which required the deprivation of her liberty, and loss of coherent speech was painful to watch. It is far from certain, but I got no sense of Sarah recognising me from church. She had her quiet periods, where we would walk companionably up and down the corridor, and raucous periods, where she got very agitated and vocal. She spoke, but for those listening it made no sense at all.

Sarah was asked if she'd like to attend the services I organised, and although she wasn't able to convey a comprehensible reply, she didn't object to being led to the lounge where I ran them. She was quite restless and occasionally left the room, but managed to find her way back. But then two things happened which were unexpected and brought great joy to her family when I told them later.

One was the hymns – clearly, for Sarah, music had an impact. When we sang the hymns she joined in. And not with her confused 'ramblings', but with all the correct lyrics from the hymns, and you could see how much she loved singing them.

Then, after the service had ended, Sarah stood up and made to leave – she paused in the corridor, stood in front of me, and said, clear as a bell: 'Thank you for that, it was a very good service.' I have to confess that I stood there with my mouth open for a few seconds, so unexpected was this. Then she turned, set off down the corridor with her usual vigour, and resumed her incomprehensible dialogue with no one in particular.

This has stayed with me, and is a constant reminder of the person 'within'. Even though Sarah appeared to no longer be the person I previously knew, her former character was there, somewhere. Music, worship, and God still had a meaning to Sarah, and she deserved every opportunity to experience that meaning.

* * *

Whether short or long, all these anecdotes and experiences are such encouraging examples of people who are still able to relate to God despite their dementia having become quite advanced. They all illustrate that, despite cognition failing, God is still 'the strength of their heart' (Psalm 73:26).

8

'God knows me, therefore I am'

'I will not forget you! See, I have engraved you on the palms of my hands.'
ISAIAH 49:15–16

These accounts of expressions of faith lead me naturally to reflecting on where God fits into the lives of those living with dementia. If knowledge of God leads to worship and an awareness of ourselves, what happens when one can no longer remember either self or God? The answer lies in God's promise of always remembering and loving them, regardless of their own failing memory. Indeed, the dread of forgetting can be overcome by God's beautiful promises: 'Never will I leave you; never will I forsake you' (Hebrews 13:5). Even if we have forgotten, we still remain ourselves when he remembers us, 'I will not forget you! See, I have engraved you on the palms of my hands' (Isaiah 49:15–16).

This could be the most profound truth of all for those living with dementia: that they are loved and wanted irrespective of their physical or psychological condition. 'Human beings' value and identity are held and assured by the God who created them.'[1]

The fact that personhood has to do with God's longing to relate to us in a personal way cannot be proved analytically, but it can be lived in our relationships with others. Elizabeth MacKinlay reminds us that who we become is shaped by those we encounter, but that nevertheless our real identity is sustained by God 'who in Christ is with us and for us, particularly in our darkest hours of need'.[2] Surely, if God knew us when we were still in the womb (Psalm 139) and has plans for us to prosper (Jeremiah 29:11), then neurological decline is not going to separate us from his love? In fact, as this book has discovered, lives that are touched by profound forms of dementia can still have meaning and continuing purpose for both the person living with it and those caring for them.

It is true that the Bible does not specifically mention dementia, but there are lasting principles that help us to understand illness and disease, and help us to respond in God-honouring ways. One of these principles is that God has a purpose in all that happens. The psalmist wrote: 'I cry out to God Most High, to God who fulfils his purpose for me' (Psalm 57:2, ESV). Even while recognising that God had a purpose, the psalmist still cried out to God in his need. This leads to the recognition that the more we get to know God, the more we can trust him, even when we don't understand why he does what he does. As Jennifer Bute discovered, once we recognise that in his infinite wisdom, he has a purpose that he can use in dementia, there is no problem affirming his love and power. As John Swinton puts it: 'To misunderstand the nature and purpose of God's memory is to misunderstand the practices of God in the lives of people living with dementia.'[3] To be remembered by God is to be known, held, and loved by God. God's part in all this gets to the heart of the matter. MacKinlay quotes the following rather beautiful story:

> *An elderly lady living with dementia paced the corridors of the nursing home restlessly – repeating over and over just one word. The staff were disconcerted, but no one seemed quite sure how to calm her and put her mind at rest. In fact, they were at a loss to understand the reason for her distress. The word she kept repeating was 'God'. One day a nurse walked with her up and down the corridor until eventually in a flash of inspiration she asked the lady, 'Are you afraid that you will forget God?' 'Yes, yes!' she replied emphatically. The nurse was then able to say to*

her, 'You know, even if you should forget God, he will not forget you. He has promised that.' For this lady who was forgetting many things, and was aware of it, that assurance was all she needed to hear. She immediately became more peaceful, and that particular behaviour of pacing restlessly ceased. She was responding positively to care which extended beyond the needs of body and mind – care of the human spirit.[4]

In my conversation with Swinton, he reaffirmed that basically all types of dementia are brain damage. So, the part of your brain that has been damaged will determine what you can or cannot understand. But the amount you can understand is not the criteria for the amount of the love that God gives you. People do get very concerned when the person living with dementia cannot articulate their faith in the way they used to, or can't talk about Jesus in the way we expect them to talk, and wonder how they can possibly have faith. But this thinking is actually limiting God – it is simply not true that in order to love God he requires you to have a whole brain, and if you have damaged one part of your brain then God will stop communicating with you! These ideas echo Joanna Collicutt's thoughts in part 2 of *Thinking of You*, which is entitled 'Thinking about the person with dementia'.[5]

He finished by saying he just trusts in God's unfailing love, and that we, as followers of Jesus, need to help people experience that. If they can articulate that, then that's great, but God is not determined by our words. As John Dunlop puts it: 'God sees all of us as broken and in need of his love. How we are broken doesn't matter.'[6]

Our essential identity, who we are in Christ, is safe in him. As human beings, this condition will bring changes to how we express ourselves and our faith. But God's love for us does not change. Surely when John wrote, 'God so loved the world' (John 3:16), he meant everyone? This is not to discount the pain of losing our memory. There is much suffering for those experiencing living with dementia, and certainly things are completely changed. But human beings experiencing dementia do not dissolve. They remain tightly held within the memories of God himself.

A continual theme from scripture is that in suffering and darkness there is joy, hope, and growth (see Romans 5:1–5). We only need to look at the story of God's people in the Old Testament to see this pattern at work. For the Christian believer, the scriptures tell us again and again that in suffering our trust in God is strengthened as we become increasingly filled with the hope of faith. There is a tension between hope and sadness, and lament is involved. Psalms 3, 13, 22, 42, and 60 are just a few of the lament psalms. These psalms teach us that it is never wrong to cry out to God. He hears us and welcomes us close to him. At its core, lamentation is an act of faith, for God is the only one who can do something about our pain. In our weakness, we call out to God knowing he is there and that he knows and remembers us. At the same time, lamenting is almost always a hopeful practice, because it is directed to God and so can bring us back to God and to feeling his love, even in the midst of the brokenness, the sadness.

And of course, it is not only the one living with dementia who is crying out for help, but their supporters too. A partner of a person living with dementia has two main roles, as partner and as caregiver. The question partners ask is: 'From where does our help come?' (see Psalm 121). Lamenting can turn the grief and guilt into strength to fight evil, together with a God whose empathy and love stays with a partner in her or his loneliness and grief.

Kenneth Carder takes this thought even further, as he reflects on life with his wife Linda, whose dementia is advanced:

> *Linda's discipleship and vocation are now simply to be and to receive the love of others. Although some tasks may become burdensome, Linda is never a burden. She is a means of grace, God's presence and power to transform others who choose to be present with her. Her presence with us in her dependency is teaching us what it means to be a person made in the divine image and loved by God, and she is enabling us to grow more fully in love for God and neighbour. She is wooing us to love one another as Christ loves us.*[7]

The apostle Paul stresses the importance of being known by God: 'Now, however, that you have come to know God, or *rather to be known by God*, how can you turn back again to the weak and beggarly elemental principles?' (Galatians 4:8–9, NRSV; emphasis added). Paul also visits this theme in his first letter to the Corinthians: 'For now we see in a mirror dimly, but then face to face. Now I know in part; then I shall know fully, *even as I have been fully known*' (1 Corinthians 13:12, ESV; emphasis added).

It is moving to reflect on more words from Christine Bryden, who despite living with dementia herself, is still able to boldly proclaim:

> *Christian confessions and creeds start with the words 'I believe', not 'I remember'. Even though I may no longer remember God, I will trust him to hold me in his memory until that glorious day of resurrection, when each facet of my personality will be expressed to the full. This unique essence of me is at my core, and this is what will remain with me to the end. I will be perhaps even more truly 'me' than I have ever been.*

Though dementia may strip away mental capacities, it is a reminder of our utter reliance on God. For those affected by dementia this reminder may take the form of surprising experiences of spiritual growth, even in the midst of deepest loss and suffering. We should never doubt that someone living with dementia can still love, if we think of love as being other-person centred. A 'thank you' offered in response to kindness or a smile when prayed for or touched may well be acts of love. As faith is a gift of God bestowed on a human being (Romans 4:16), and we know that someone living with dementia is a human being, it follows that they can still receive that gift. For people whose cognition means they live in the moment, we can expect to see 'works' of a moment.[8] Another reminder comes in Psalm 139:7–8, which states there is nowhere beyond the reach of God and no state too low to be raised up by him: 'Where can I go from your Spirit? Where can I flee from your presence?'

The following beautiful reflections, based on Psalm 139, come from a daughter whose mother is now living with advanced dementia.

> *In so many ways, I'm unable to communicate with her. Remembering my favourite Psalm 139, I cry out to God. I ask him to speak into her heart, which can't process much of anything other than meal time, a brief card game of War, or a short visit with her sister before she falls asleep again. I ask God to touch her deep within her soul, to give her his assurance and peace. When she's awake, I sing with her all manner of songs – from silly songs about crocodiles to beautiful hymns about God's faithfulness. Sometimes, in the middle of the night I hear her singing 'Take me out to the ball game' or humming 'A mighty fortress is our God'. Mom has returned, ever so briefly, and it's a very sweet gift to me...*
>
> *My mother can't call on Jesus to help her. She's no longer clear who he is. She cannot seek God for peace. She cannot pray to him. She cannot cry out to him – at least not in any verbal way. Who among us has contemplated the end of our days and considered we might not be able to pray aloud?...*
>
> *[God] knows absolutely everything about my mother. He knows all about her lying down, which is most of her time (Psalm 139:2–3). He knows about her anxious thoughts and understands her words that we no longer understand (Psalm 139:4). He is behind and before her (Psalm 139:5)... When I settle my heart, I know the only thing changed is my mother's memory. God has not changed... He can minister to her soul despite her lacking knowledge of him...*
>
> *I find deep hope and comfort that although I can't provide for my mother's deep need for peace, God can. Dementia is not too dark for the God who is fully present with her on this dim and murky path. The psalmist concludes by asking God to lead him in the way everlasting (Psalm 139:24). So too I ask God to*

gently, in his time, lead her to her everlasting home and into his glorious light.[9]

Reflecting that cognitive competence is not essential to encounter the grace of God led me once again to the writings of Henri Nouwen. His thoughts on the poverty of the cognitively disabled could so easily have been written about the poverty of those living with dementia:

> *I've seen that God speaks to us through the poor. And the people I live with here are really poor. Not in an economic way, but they are empty. They don't have much capacity to analyse things. They're poor in terms of even their emotions at times. But their heart is open to God. They may be stripped of a lot of human skills, but in their poverty they are open to God. Their heart – and by heart, I mean the centre of their being – is so poor in a way that God can dwell there.*[10]

René Descartes most famous saying ('I think, therefore I am') can be further adapted as the dementia journey continues. 'I think, therefore I am' becomes 'I feel and relate, therefore I am', which becomes 'I know God, therefore I am', which finally becomes 'God knows me, therefore I am'. All these statements are true, but perhaps for someone moving towards the final stages of dementia, the last is the most pertinent of all. Christine Bryden suggests that as she lives with dementia, forgetting the past and unaware of the future, she hopes others will understand and help her experience a relationship with God in the here and now, suggesting that Galatians 3:28 could be paraphrased: 'There is no longer cognitive competence or incapacity, for we are all one in Christ Jesus.'

I am praying that those living with dementia will be able to move from 'I think, therefore I am' to 'God knows me, therefore I am'. This will only be possible if those supporting them begin to realise that loss of memory does not mean loss of personhood, and if the church embraces them fully as part of the worshipping community. I wrote in chapter one of how Jennifer Bute is inspired by *kintsukuroi* to embrace her flaws, seeing how beautifully God can repair her. But the artist Makoto

Fujimura takes this a step further: 'Wouldn't we be a more inclusive church if we simply allowed broken people to gather, and did not try to "fix" them, but simply to love and behold them, contemplating the shapes that broken pieces can inspire?'[11] In other words, we should realise that those living with dementia are fully part of the community, and deserve our welcome, love, and support, just as they are.

I believe the church is only truly fulfilling its calling to mission when it includes those whom most consider weak, vulnerable, or marginalised. This is certainly implicit in Paul's words in 1 Corinthians 12:12–31, in particular verse 24: 'God has so arranged the body, giving the greater honour to the inferior member' (NRSV). In Matthew 25:34–46 we learn that when we care for those the world considers strangers, we are caring for Jesus himself. As John Swinton puts it: 'Such acts of friendship towards strangers are acts of worship, in the sense that Jesus places "the outcast" under divine protection and his followers under divine obligation to offer hospitality to the stranger and outcast in society.'[12] Perhaps the most poignant thought of all is that 'in many ways the deepest revelation of the dementia journey is that it is a journey from the mind into the heart'.[13] And it is this journey that we are privileged to share as we support those living with dementia to continue to find meaning in 'the land of forgetfulness', as they experience the eternal truth that 'God knows me, therefore I am'.

Finally, I am praying this book may encourage the wider church to accept and see those living with dementia in a new light and understand that faith can still be experienced through senses, emotions, relationships, and the arts, even when cognition fails. My prayer is that the church will realise the truth that we are called to be God's community in which the marginalised, including those living with dementia, are welcomed, involved, and strengthened. And it is this vital issue of how the church could and should be involved with those living with dementia that Frances addresses in the second part of this book.

PART II

How can churches better support families living with dementia?

Frances Attwood

9

Learning about the needs

'Who knows but that you have come to your royal position for such a time as this?'
ESTHER 4:14

My interest in the role churches play in supporting families living with dementia began when I was running music groups for these families living in the community. I noticed how both carer and cared-for relaxed for that brief period, entering into the fun of singing songs from their youth, temporarily forgetting the challenges of living with dementia. I saw how those living with dementia were all able to engage at whatever level, and the carers stepped out of their supporting role to sing or play for their own pleasure. One carer commented, 'I love being recognised by name, not just as his carer.'

I also observed how, within only a few weeks of attending, the carers made a beeline for each other, recognising that there were others who fully understood the daily challenges of supporting their family member. It was a safe space, where apparently bizarre behaviours were not a major cause of concern or embarrassment, and where the priority was on what people could do, rather than what was lost.

I soon learned that there were few other opportunities for social engagement for these families. Carers' lives appeared to be engulfed by the supporting role they had involuntarily taken on, and as families, they became increasingly isolated, only going out to attend medical appointments and other essential engagements. This caused me to wonder if churches could provide the opportunities for stimulation, connection, and support these families so clearly needed. I began to research the national provision of care from both the state and churches.

Although my original motivation came from these experiences as a therapist running community music groups, as I have been writing this book I have changed role several times, which has been useful in offering me different perspectives. When I retired as a music therapist, I undertook an MA in applied theology at Moorlands Bible College, specialising in chaplaincy. This gave me the opportunity and privilege of time to reflect on my former practice as well as considering the theological basis for regarding people with dementia and the role of churches. While studying, I was volunteering at Immanuel Church, a real luxury after leading sessions, as I had the time to observe what was happening and enjoy interacting with the families that attended the reminiscence sessions.

So while I was researching for my dissertation, I could not become purely theoretical; I had to remain grounded in what I was seeing every week. It was also helpful to be able to interview leaders of older people's ministry in other local churches and the coordinator of activities across part of the county to gain some different perspectives of what churches have to offer. Even at that time I was hoping to reach a wider audience with what I was learning, so I was grateful to have the consent from all those who contributed to my research under ethical supervision to be able to publish what they shared.

Of course, I was only looking at a small number of churches, and it is impossible to generalise from what I learned; however, I feel it can be helpful as a snapshot of what is going on in some places to encourage other churches to reflect on their own practice. It was only after completing my research, and at this point taking on the leadership of reminiscence sessions at Immanuel, that I undertook the Anna Chaplaincy training, giving me yet one more slant on ministry in this area.

So, as you read, you may detect some shifts in outlook according to the work I have been doing with people with dementia and their families.

The national picture

There are currently estimated to be 982,000 people in the United Kingdom who have dementia, although this only includes those with a formal diagnosis. Many are supported by family members, of whom 36% spend more than 100 hours a week in their caring role. Of these carers, one in three are themselves over 80 years of age. However, a third of people living with dementia live alone.[1]

As well as the direct challenges of the condition, problems for families living with dementia are compounded by cuts to funding of social care. Moreover, some organisations require a formal diagnosis before someone can attend their activities or courses. Currently, it can take up to two years to obtain a diagnosis, which also delays access to financial support or to medication that can reduce symptoms in the early stages of some forms of the condition. So, there is very little provision for social connection for those living with dementia, and the few opportunities for carers to have respite come at a high price.

Despite the demands on them, family carers largely feel insufficiently supported themselves. Current means-testing does not as easily identify needs arising from deficiencies in cognitive functioning as those resulting from physical disability. Consequently, someone living with dementia may not meet the criteria to justify carer's allowance. Meanwhile, most energy and funding have gone into medical research to find the cause and potential cure of dementia, rather than the support of those living with the condition now and the known detrimental effects of loneliness.

Some of the issues facing these families are not unique to those living with dementia. For example, lack of transport compounded with mobility problems affects many older people or those with disabilities. With the additional difficulties facing families living with dementia, there are even fewer openings for being actively involved in their communities.

For those who have a Christian faith, there are further challenges arising from the disconnection from their faith community. With memory failings, it is harder to retain the assurance of God's faithfulness without the regular support of a church, and church services may no longer be reassuring due to an unfamiliar style of worship. Practical obstacles to maintaining relationships with a local church may deny both people living with dementia and their carers the support of a loving fellowship. It can be all too easy for these families to 'fall off the radar' once regular attendance has become too difficult.

It appears that church support across the United Kingdom is very patchy. There are instances of churches which offer accessible activities and make provision for these families; however, these appear to be the exception rather than the rule. Within some Anglican dioceses, most notably Lichfield Diocese, there is a developed programme of training in awareness and support; however, this is not replicated nationally.[2] Some other denominations, such as the Methodist Church, Salvation Army, and Church of Scotland, have produced resources for making services more dementia-friendly. Anna Chaplains, a chaplaincy specifically focused on older people's spiritual support, sometimes have specialist knowledge and interest in dementia, and they would certainly encounter and include people with this condition in their ministry. Some national Christian organisations, such as Pilgrims' Friend Society and Faith in Later Life,[3] are encouraging and resourcing churches to be able to reach out to people living with dementia, but it still seems that generally across the United Kingdom, churches do not currently have a strategic plan and developed ministry to families living with this condition.

The church's potential to provide support

Churches, however, are ideally placed, being both historically and geographically in the centre of most communities, to offer care, connection, and social and spiritual support to these families. Many churches have a track record within their local communities of offering services, such as food banks or parent-and-toddler groups, and are therefore known and trusted. In most residential areas, whether hamlet or city, there are local churches. This is important as they are likely to be reasonably accessible for those for whom transport is an issue. Churches usually have buildings that can accommodate groups, and have regular attenders, many of whom are committed to service and frequently volunteer their time. Moreover, those who have a personal faith see their responsibility to care for others within and beyond their congregations. So, most churches already have the resources necessary to provide support for families living with dementia.

Research into local church support

To understand more about what churches offer, what people living with dementia and their family carers desire, and how provision could be improved, I studied four local churches. I made a conscious decision to investigate the needs of both the person living with dementia and their family carer, which although different in some ways, appear to me to be so enmeshed that one cannot be considered without the other.

I was volunteering in one of the churches in my study, Immanuel Church, Southbourne, so had the opportunity to learn first-hand from families living with dementia who attended this church, as well as the minister to older people, Sally Nevitt, and the leader of a weekly reminiscence session. In order to gain a wider perspective, I interviewed the leaders from three other local churches that are committed to older people's ministry, including those living with dementia. I was also fortunate enough to gain the insights of a coordinator in a Christian agency which has a contract from the local authority to organise activities for seniors throughout the county.

Of course, not all people living with dementia are older and not all older people develop dementia. In fact, two of the people I observed had young onset forms of the condition. While I framed my questions to my participants specifically asking about dementia, they often responded by talking about older people in general. So, some of the comments I have captured might give the impression that I make no distinction. In fact, provision for younger people living with dementia is likely to be even less, as they are in a minority.

I was most anxious to hear from people living with dementia themselves, but feared that, for some, interviews would be too demanding, so I instead noted their comments and my own observations of their responses. The family carers completed questionnaires, as they would struggle to find enough time alone to be interviewed. However, there were two former carers whose relative had died and who were willing to talk about their experience. They were able to reflect on what they would have wished for, as well as what support they felt their local churches had given them. When I asked the agency's activity coordinator about what local church support there was for families living with dementia throughout the county, her immediate response was: 'Not a lot!' Among most of the church leaders, while there was clearly a concern for seniors in general, there was no specific focus on dementia. They were open to the potential of having people living with dementia attend their events, but there was little training and few resources to meet their specific needs. There was a feeling that activities and events targeted towards people living with dementia needed the expertise of professionals.

Immanuel Church, by contrast, stood out for the extent of their work in this area. They had an appointed older people's minister, Sally Nevitt, and offered a whole week's programme of events and activities that were dementia-friendly (accessible and supported by a team that had had some training), and three activities specifically aimed at people living with dementia and memory loss. At the time of doing my research, I was volunteering at the reminiscence afternoons run by the church, so was able to observe and interact with the guests living with dementia, a few family carers who remained for the whole session, and, occasionally, professional carers.

As I learned about the disparity of provision between different churches, I began to consider possible reasons for this variation. I explore this in the next few chapters and the potential for learning from the experience of a thriving ministry.

10

Is this the job of the church?

> *We are God's handiwork, created in Christ Jesus to do good works, which God prepared in advance for us to do.*
> EPHESIANS 2:10

One potential explanation for different practices between churches is the various beliefs held about what the role of the church is. The question concerns whether the church should primarily be making disciples or focusing on demonstrating love in acts of care and justice – or a mixture of the two.

From the perspective of the whole of scripture, God has always had a mission to establish his kingdom and redeem the whole of creation, reflecting his concern for the weak, the vulnerable, the broken, and the victims of injustice. The nature of his kingdom has been indicated through his covenant relationship with ancient Israel and has now been inaugurated through Christ's death and resurrection. The church's mission is thus framed within this ultimate and universal story, providing a preview of the future perfect fulfilment of Christ's reign as king over all. The church is thus engaged in God's redemption of 'the totality of human beings in every sphere of their lives',[1] and in instilling hope in the realisation of the promised future. This narrative of the church's mission appears especially helpful to those struggling with dementia, in need of practical support now, and also hope to sustain them.

This comprehensive understanding of the church's responsibility as citizens of God's kingdom also suggests partnership with those outside the church, wherever there is the possibility of collaborating in our distinctive ways.

How might this work out in practice?

There was some ambivalence among those I interviewed as to the purpose of their ministry:

'There is a real aspect of really taking care of them and loving and accepting them and being there for them. I think churches still need to sit up and address some of the pastoral needs for their older sector.'

'There's the spiritual side of meeting people's needs and there's the social aspect as well, so I think it should go hand in hand... As a church, we want to be different from, say, a charity... we want it to... meet people's spiritual needs, but also, we're not sort of social workers either. So, it's sort of striking a balance, and it's got to be really purposeful and clear what you want to achieve for the people, and what the needs really are... If it's in the church I'd like there to be a bit more Christian content, really, than just a social group.'

There feels to be some natural overlap between pastoral care, looking after the needs of a church's congregation, and the care of those outside the church. In some cases, long-term members, even those in active ministry, may develop dementia, and they and their families will require an increasing amount of support, even beyond the point when they are able to attend services and events. Some may be less active, but still have a strong allegiance to the church. Others may have a more tenuous relationship, but still come under the parish or belong to the local community.

The term 'pastoral', though, implies a specifically spiritual attention, different from what, for example, social services can offer. The interest is in the whole person's welfare, not just attending to physical issues or finding pragmatic solutions to problems. Part of caring for our neighbour, even those outside the church, may be offering this spiritual support while giving practical care.

One family carer's comment reflects an appreciation of this Christian aspect of the support provided:

'Although I've stopped going to church, I still found it – I liked it, yeah. I liked the Christian input in there. It was good.'

This ministry can also be a witness beyond those living with dementia to wider family, volunteers, and the local community. Despite initially thinking they would not have any funeral or memorial, the grieving extended family and friends of a guest at the reminiscence sessions sought a way to honour and treasure his life. Through deep conversations and careful liaison, the church provided a meaningful, personalised memorial service attended by a large number. Legacies from past church members also reflected the level of appreciation for what the church had offered in terms of practical care and love. A local secular agency gave a generous donation to the church in recognition of what it was doing in the community. So the impact can go far beyond the immediate family.

Offering support to those living with dementia beyond the church, at a time when few others are reaching out to them, can potentially attract people to explore faith. Outreach to families living with dementia can be, for some, the beginning of a journey to become part of the church community, and from there to seek answers to deeper spiritual questions. I heard a professional carer say: 'I don't go to church, but if I did, I would go to this one!' Seeing love in action can open opportunities to share more about the God we serve.

But isn't this the job of the state?

Another question that arises from the needs of families living with dementia is whether it is, in fact, the church's responsibility to provide the support. Shouldn't it be the state, as this is a health and social care issue? As we are all too aware, the NHS is struggling to meet the health needs of the whole population, and social services have always been given lower priority in terms of funding. But, whereas interventions of the NHS or social services may be the most appropriate to address the physical, practical, and, in some cases, acute mental health decline, in the later stages of dementia, it is hard to see how they can offer the social, let alone the spiritual, support needed by families, sometimes over many years.

Respite care or residential accommodation may be beyond the financial means of many families, and if, by providing support from the earliest stages of the condition, churches can delay or even prevent the need for these measures, this is to be preferred by these families. Scientific research has shown that social interaction and stimulation, such as could be provided by churches, can help to delay the symptoms of dementia, and the negative impact of lockdowns during the pandemic on health and well-being endorses the importance of connection. Family carers save the UK Government 'an estimated £184 billion pounds a year, which is equivalent to a second NHS',[2] so it is also in the national interest to save carers from 'burn out', which churches may be able to do, simply by supporting them.

There are secular charities that focus on dementia, like the Alzheimer's Society and Dementia UK, but it is important to distinguish between what kinds of aid these charities deliver from what they do not offer. The Alzheimer's Society has several aims: to provide information about dementia, to campaign for better provision, to offer an online forum for all concerned in every aspect of dementia, to raise money for research, and to change society's perceptions of dementia. While it does encourage community initiatives, it no longer funds local support groups but relies on volunteers. Dementia UK provides a more personalised advisory service to families and emotional support as the condition progresses.

Both organisations are important and influential, but they cannot give the connection with community which is so needed by families living with dementia. Other, smaller organisations produce helpful resources, recreational opportunities, offer online forums, and advise institutions in how to create more dementia-friendly environments – all good, and steps in the right direction of improving quality of life, but still limited in their reach and impact. The sheer number of churches and their location within communities suggest that they are in the best position to make a real difference.

Churches have a mandate to love their neighbours. Throughout scripture we see how God has a particular concern for the marginalised, the poor, and the afflicted. If we are to emulate our heavenly Father, this should characterise us, too. The sort of care that churches can offer goes beyond that of any organisation, whether government or charity, in loving families living with dementia. I will go on to consider what sort of support is wanted by these families and how churches see their role in this.

11

What families living with dementia want

> *During the night Paul had a vision of a man of Macedonia standing and begging him, 'Come over to Macedonia and help us.'*
> ACTS 16:9

I wanted to learn from families living with dementia and from churches offering support to them what the needs are and how those needs might be met, and to learn from their responses what further support churches might offer. I will take each perspective separately before considering the importance of local provision (which can benefit both people living with dementia and their family carers), how significant support is to these families, and how, in the end, it is the loving care churches give that makes the difference.

People living with dementia

The comments from those who attended the reminiscence sessions tended to be general and short but overwhelmingly expressed how important they are to them:

'It's my favourite day of the week.'

'They will sometimes say, "I've had a lovely afternoon", or that they've enjoyed it. They're not very effusive, but then you wouldn't expect them to be. We know from the feedback that we get, that they appreciate coming along and there being something for them.'

'It was obviously something that he looked forward to 'cause he'd actually written it down in the book.'

'As they go out, they always say something. So, they've "really enjoyed it", or, "Thank you very much"... They are very polite in that age range, but they do say on other occasions, "Oh, I really love coming here", and, "This really, really is helpful and enjoyable." They feel part of the group, so, part of the little community.'

Relief from isolation features strongly:

'It's company, isn't it? There's only so much television you can watch.

'Without these activities, Mum would only see her carers and members of her family.'

'Opportunity for Mum to mingle with people her own age.'

'Another outlet where they can meet people and be outside their own four walls.'

For those for whom there are few opportunities to socialise, church activities or events can enable people living with dementia to remain integrated in the community.

But it is also the need for **accessible activities or events**, with the right level of support. Previous engagement in groups may no longer be possible.

'There aren't that many resources locally for them to be taking part in things socially.'

'They may not be able to do activities they used to do. They may not be able to attend those.'

'Just because they've got this diagnosis doesn't mean that they just have to stay at home.'

'You do get some people who fall between the gaps really... who haven't got a diagnosis... So, by opening up our groups to anybody, it just meant that actually you could support those people.'

Providing **mental stimulation** is important:

'The chance to participate in something that's very much aimed at their abilities, so that they get some sense of satisfaction of participating.'

'Giving them something to do that stimulates their mind.'

'All designed to bring out the conversation and just give the brain a little bit of a gentle, gentle workout.'

'Mental stimulation slows the progress of dementia, so singing, quizzes, and craft exercises all contribute to improving mental states.'

'It's all about maintaining skills'.

I observed that, despite some abilities being lost or at least in decline, because there was a range of activities offered in the reminiscence sessions, there was usually something that guests could still manage, in some cases very well. For example, one guest could still tackle complex arithmetic, another retained her hand skills as a former florist, yet another could recite poetry learned in her youth. For this man, it was doing word searches:

'When he went in, what he would do would be a word search. He could literally sit down and get on with that, and no one should talk to him during that time because that was his thing that he did.'

This facilitation and preservation of skills chimes with national studies which show that active engagement helps to improve memory and thinking skills and even reduce cognitive decline for people with mild to moderate dementia. It enables them to experience an improved quality of life and communication. NHS England recommends cognitive stimulation therapy (CST) for people who have just received a dementia diagnosis, and it is provided by many NHS trusts. As an Admiral nurse working with carers of people living with dementia, Jackie Tuppen developed a model of maintenance CST which she called COGS Clubs; some COGS Clubs are run by churches, guided by Jackie.[1]

To discover that they could still succeed in these abilities was an important counter to awareness of failure in other areas. Having an experience of success and being enabled to contribute to the group made the guests feel valued and enhanced their confidence. This is so different from the general perception in society of people living with dementia as unable to do anything.

I was struck by the fact that **meeting with others** empowered those for whom communication had become limited. In the reminiscence sessions, the guests were seated at small tables, usually only six people per table. Because the volunteers and more articulate guests maintained a flow of chatter, those who had little speech could still contribute a remark or join in with laughter at a joke. It seemed a wonderful way to enable them to continue to be socially integrated.

Similarly, within the familiar and supportive environment of the church café, people could continue to enjoy being with friends and share in the pleasure of eating together, without having to be anxious about what to do. One woman with short-term memory problems was regularly confused about where to sit or even what she was doing in the café.

Being with church friends, who could reassure and direct her, transformed the experience into a relaxed social occasion.

Churches can **fill some of the gaps in provision** within their community:

'... just needed that little bit of earlier intervention and help them feel like there was some kind of support out there.'

'It's a continuous support structure that's part of people's daily living and that they can rely upon.'

'Part of what we wanted to do, particularly with Memory Lanes, was to have them across the conurbation and using as many different days of the week as possible.'

'Most clubs stop over the holidays... people need a break, but the families and people with a memory loss don't.'

What churches offer can also **give hope and a sense of control** in circumstances that might feel bleak:

'It's interacting with other people... giving them something to do that stimulates their mind... I think it helps them to see that life's not over.'

'Something they can participate in, and feel good about the fact that they participated in something, despite their growing awareness of having memory loss or dementia.'

'To feel that they're included, there's still a place for them.'

'They link into memories that improve their well-being.'

'I feel normal.' [Comment from a feedback book]

Another response I heard frequently was **the importance of the familiar**. Familiar structures and content of activities provide a sense of safety and belonging for people living with dementia, particularly with short-term memory loss:

'I think it was the structure of it, that he knew, almost knew, where he was going to sit, and who he was going to sit with.'

'I realised how important the liturgy… is to people… because they know it… B. used to love… the songs, and particularly the liturgy, that he knew by heart.'

'So that people don't feel like worship's alien to them… particularly for people with dementia… it could feel very isolated if there's not one song or hymn that you're familiar with.'

'He'll come here because this is a place that feels safe and is familiar to him… even though he was suggested one more local.'

'My wife feels very comfortable in these surroundings.'

I observed how people living with dementia developed strong relationships in the reminiscence sessions, both with other guests and with the leaders and regular volunteers. Names were frequently forgotten, but the important thing was recognising familiar faces and to feel at ease with each other.

'We had a new lady start, and the daughter had told me how bad her short-term memory was. But then… this lady's second week, she came in the room, and she automatically just charged almost with her walker towards the table and then spotted someone she remembered from the week before and said, "I'm going to sit there. That's my friend."'

I noted how, at Immanuel Church, many people came in every day of the week to the various activities they offered or to the friendly café.

Hence, the whole place felt to be one of safety and familiarity, where they knew church staff and volunteers and were known by them. In a culture in which we have lost much of the sense of local community, this appeared to be such a healthy atmosphere, and enabled families living with dementia to remain integrated.

One of the features of the reminiscence sessions was the amount of **enjoyment and laughter**. Evidently, people who had attended the sessions left with a feeling of happiness:

'We can see from their body language, and, you know, the conversation we have as they're going, they're better than when they came in.'

'We hear a lot of laughter come from it, and I think that's a good sign they're obviously having fun.'

As I write this, I am reminded of a comment I heard only this week: *'When I came, I was feeling very down. I can't walk now, and I find that very hard. But this session has really cheered me up.'*

It is easy to underestimate the worth of pleasurable experience, but it is important for the mental well-being of those living with dementia who may struggle with confusion, anxiety, and distress at lost abilities. It is the emotion that is most likely to be retained while the memory of the content of the event may not, so, if guests leave with the feeling of joy, this will last beyond the session.

'They might not be [able to] engage that much, but, actually, being in that safe and happy environment, obviously, can help affect their mood and their emotions for the day.'

'They'll go away feeling very happy and positive.'

Family carers' experience

What came across from the family carers was the **emotional intensity of the experience of caring.**

'I was looking for support wherever I could get it.'

'A lot of the time I was very near the edge, didn't realise it at the time, but… if people are kind to you, you'll be in tears… it's realising the emotional level that the carers are at with it all.'

'I was getting very down and tired, it was quite hard… I had this real fear of being shut in and not being able to go and do anything… and, of course, that came to pass.'

Carers expressed a strong **desire for some respite**:

'I think the main thing that was missing… and eventually, when he really began not to communicate very well, was visiting.'

'They are very thankful, particularly if they have been able to leave someone. It gives them a break.'

'I needed someone to come and just sit with him… I had a sitter… so I could go to the women's fellowship… at the time I had the finance to be able to pay someone to come and do that.'

I was aware that paying for professional respite care would not be financially possible for all carers. The support and events their churches offered gave them **some time out of the caring role:**

'Lovely group for me, too.'

'They're not responsible for this time.'

'The afternoon where I get to have a rest, too.'

'He [a carer] had really enjoyed just getting out and just having someone else organise things and so that he could sit and enjoy.'

'Opportunity for me to have my wife be independent of me in a safe environment for a couple of hours.'

'Should it be a situation where she [the relative with dementia] just sees carers at home and he [the carer] needed to get out, he could come to the group... and just enjoy the company of one of our carers' groups.'

'Good all-round afternoon for both my husband and myself.'

However, there is a desire for **more than just respite**:

'It would be nice if it [the church] could provide a counselling service for carers.'

'I would have liked more individual support. There was one week when I broke down crying, it just got to me... I did think that, you know, maybe I could have had a bit of follow up there... I think it would have been nice to have a bit more support for the carers. Just to express how [frustrated] you are and how upset you get.'

Just the simple act of **giving time to listen** to these feelings could help to release stress and exhaustion.

'One of the things... which would have helped me particularly was to have a prayer ministry after the morning service... that sort of practical "Let's get down and pray about it now" thing would have helped me a great deal.'

Although there were local carer support groups, the challenge for these carers was finding someone to look after their family member while they attended.

Meeting with other families living with dementia is part of the solution to isolation:

'Being around other people who understand, you know, what they're going through.'

[In response to the question, 'What do you value about this activity/event?'] *'Meeting up with friendly people.'*

It does not require much effort to provide **opportunities for carers to meet**, as well as those they are supporting.

Family carers are really heartened to **glimpse some of the intact memories and abilities** of their relative in response to the stimulation of the sessions:

'Once they start coming, they come, because they love to see their family member laughing, singing, doing things that they haven't been doing at home.'

'I think it's just seeing the way people can come alive and the fact when you interact with them and they're responding, and there's always those little stories that come up of someone who's not spoken for weeks but they're interacting… and the carers are then blessed.'

'She remembered, "Actually, I want to be there"… I fed that back to the daughter, and she was just bowled over, because she just never thought that her mum would actually remember anyone from the week before.'

'There was this glow on her face that he was engaging. And that's so much of the feedback from the relatives, that they're seeing – this reaction from their loved ones that they used to see before.'

In some instances, too, the stimulation of attending events and activities facilitates **easier relationships between family members**, as the carer can temporarily relax and not feel solely responsible for their relative's well-being, while the renewed engagement of their relative can spill over into life at home:

'One of the family members just said to me, "Oh, he really loves this particular activity, do you know where I can get a book of that?"'

'If their loved one has had a good time… and been given a good experience, I think, when they go home, they're probably a bit easier to manage, so, I see it as being of benefit, hopefully, to both.'

However, there were **some negative experiences:**

'For me, I struggled a bit, I found that – I am a person that needs to be doing something, and I struggled to sit there and watch other people doing… It distressed me to see so many people in that condition.'

It requires sensitivity and attention to the carer's needs as much as the needs of those living with dementia. I have found some carers spontaneously assisting with the reminiscence sessions, and some others find it helpful to offer their time after losing their relative to dementia.

Perspective of church leaders

The interviews with the five church leaders and the activity coordinator of the Christian agency raised some of the wider issues regarding provision for these families. One is the fact that there are an **increasing number of families needing support:**

'It's a challenge of our time as the population gets a lot older and diagnoses become better and more frequent.'

Another issue is that dementia may only be a part of a complex set of difficulties facing these families:

'Sometimes they are living with memory loss, but they are also a carer of someone else who's got an even greater additional need... dementia is just that one aspect of an additional need that they might have... They are dealing with ill health, with memory loss, isolation, depression.'

Often there are **physical and sensory issues** which need consideration in addition to cognitive decline:

'I used to take him to church. I had a wheelchair thing in the back, and I would take him... and that was a real effort physically, but then they would come out and push him into church for me, and that sort of thing, which helped.'

'They had a good loop, and I think that's important for people with dementia, that they do have a good sound system, so at least they can hear properly what's going on.'

A telling comment from the activity coordinator indicates how the needs of these families, often **long-term** and not really catered for within our social care system, can be provided by churches:

'... those kind of services that might prevent them getting to that crisis point of social services. Social services can't deal with the non-crisisy stuff any more.'

A church leader agreed: *'Nobody's ready, any of the council services.'*

From her previous role of working as a professional carer with older people, the activity coordinator observed:

'That just really showed me, actually, how many people that were out there and just didn't have a voice and had just been forgotten about.'

Churches, being located in the heart of communities, may be in a position to keep the connection with older people, including those living with dementia, and ensure that their voice will be heard and that they are not forgotten.

The specific issues for Christian families

One of the areas I investigated was church support of families living with dementia who had a Christian faith.

Clearly, there were **challenges around attendance**. These comments come from a family carer:

'Sometimes she [a sitter] would stay an extra hour or two so that I could go to church. There were many weeks when I couldn't.'

'A lot of the time in the service I was concentrating on keeping an eye on him.'

This response from a church leader, who had also had a personal experience of caring for a family member living with dementia, expresses the importance of the **connection with church being maintained**:

'If you have faith, the church is an integral part of your life. If suddenly your dementia means you can no longer access church, that's a huge loss for you. But it's a devastating loss for your loved one, because now they've lost their support structure at a time that they need it desperately.'

Another carer had been disappointed with the lack of provision in her mother's church:

'Mum's faith is very important to her, and our local church does not offer any activities or support. She keeps all the prayer handouts she gets on Tuesdays and looks through them many times.'

Evidently, **the Christian element** of church support was highly significant for this woman. Another carer said, in answer to the question 'What did the fact that it was a church signify for you?', *'Certainly did for Dad, cause he was a church-goer.'*

Another carer shared the story of her husband who had been in ministry himself, and how, with the church's loving support, he was able to continue taking Communion services when he had begun to develop dementia. She said, *'That was very important to him.'* This particular church had evidently supported this man's engagement, even to the extent of enabling him to continue in ministry as long as possible.

Local provision

For both those living with dementia and their family carers, it is important that the provision is local – one of the reasons that **churches are in a good position to offer support**:

'Oh, it was really important, yeah. I mean, especially for Dad, for me to just go up to the church there. And also, there was a week when I couldn't go, or I could drop him off, but I couldn't pick him up. I think somebody took him home for me. So, that wouldn't have been able to be done if, you know, we didn't live nearby.'

'A lot of people can't travel, and transport is [a] really big issue for a lot of people.'

'He's able to travel independently still, but if that comes to an end, then I think he won't get here.'

'Especially if they're coming on their own, they will need to either get local transport or a taxi or a lift. So, [the] more local it is, the better really.'

In some families, the person living with dementia used to be the only driver, so the carer is dependent on others to take their relative to activities. In one instance I observed, the wife had physical disabilities, so could not take or accompany her husband. Another couple both had dementia, but the husband was able to drive them both the short distance to the church for some years. Several of the families employed professional carers from a local agency to bring and fetch their relatives, while other guests lived near enough to walk or come on a mobility scooter. In all of these circumstances they benefited from the proximity of the church.

The importance of this provision

The overwhelming message I received from doing my research was just how much this provision was **valued** by both people living with dementia and their family carers:

'A fantastic group and we would be lost without it.'

'Pretty well all our [reminiscence] groups are full. We've got waiting lists on most of them, and the waiting lists take forever to go down… the fact that people keep coming, and they're sad when they miss it, I think speaks volumes that, actually, the groups are making a difference to them.'

'For Dad, he just loved it. It was his highlight of the week.'

'My wife looks forward to attending the weekly meetings.'

Several of the participants said they had attended the weekly activities at Immanuel Church for two to four years, and the church estimated that they have an average of 78 attendances per week at all their activities. These numbers speak for themselves.

While not all churches may be in a position to offer such an extensive programme of dementia-friendly events and activities, increasing their provision could make a big difference to local families.

Love is what matters

My questions were all regarding specific provision for families living with dementia, so it was interesting to hear the following comments, suggesting that it was the loving care that permeated through the practical activities and provision that made such an impact:

'I suppose people loved him, really... that was sort of general care, not particularly dementia... I suppose the idea that he was loved and accepted was very important... they didn't do anything specific dementia-related service.'

'He talked about [one of the church leaders]. During Covid [she] phoned him every week. And Dad would say the same thing... but she still phoned him every week. And that – it just meant the world to him. It just meant the world to him. And he could remember when I got there. Eventually he would say, "Oh yeah, I can't remember her name. What's her name?... She phoned me today." So, it was lovely.'

We all need to feel loved and to feel we are accepted and belong. How much more that is true in times of difficulty and struggle such as arise for those living with dementia. I will go on now to consider what churches are doing to demonstrate their love for families living with dementia.

12

The support churches offer

Live such good lives among the pagans that, though they accuse you of doing wrong, they may see your good deeds and glorify God on the day he visits us.

1 PETER 2:12

Ministry to people living with dementia

Apart from Immanuel Church, all the other churches I researched said they had no specific ministry to people living with dementia. However, two hosted a Christian agency to run reminiscence sessions. While the agency ran the programme, the churches provided the venue, refreshments, a team of willing volunteers, and had the backing of the leadership and enough church members for the ministry to be supported. So, although they might not have felt they were offering anything, they were certainly facilitating these sessions and extending a welcome to people living with dementia.

Moreover, these sessions were not limited to those who had a diagnosis; they were advertised and open to anyone who had memory problems. For example, Immanuel Church advertises its reminiscence afternoons as being suitable 'for those with memory loss and all types of dementia'. This broader category helps to overcome potential fear about being known to have dementia while still communicating that these sessions would be appropriate for those struggling with any of the symptoms. It also supported people who may be at an early stage of dementia. This is particularly helpful in maintaining connection with people throughout their journey with the condition, reducing the risk of becoming isolated as symptoms worsen. There was a range of attitudes among those attending the reminiscence sessions towards their own condition. One man clearly had no awareness that he had memory problems despite that being very evident as he repeated the same stories every week. In complete contrast, another had accepted her diagnosis of dementia very easily. Others described themselves as having memory problems rather than using the word 'dementia'. It felt very important that everyone was comfortable with being known to attend the sessions regardless of their different attitudes to any labels.

All the churches I studied had social programmes for seniors, to which people living with dementia were welcome. These included open cafes, community lunches, afternoon tea, craft mornings, singing sessions, entertainment spots, quizzes, and occasional 'holiday at home' events in the summer months, when other activities temporarily ceased. These activities, perhaps precisely because they were not advertised for people living with dementia, provided opportunities for them to remain part of their communities, a vital aspect of enabling them to continue to flourish.

Immanuel Church, in addition to its reminiscence sessions, ran weekly exercise classes to music, a singing group, a friendship club which comprised a simple lunch and a visiting speaker or entertainer, and a film club showing era-appropriate films – even serving ice creams in the interval! These events were not specifically aimed at people living with dementia either, but, with leaders and volunteers who were trained in dementia-awareness and a high ratio of facilitators to guests, were all accessible and provided enough support for them to attend safely and feel comfortable.

Provision for carers

I learned that, when both the church and carers felt it was safe for a family member living with dementia to attend alone, the carers could benefit from a little time to themselves. If, however, they felt it necessary to accompany their relative, they were welcome to attend. Some, I observed at the reminiscence sessions, would stay long enough to make sure their relative was happily settled, then leave; others might return before the end of the session. So, there was flexibility according to the situation.

I noticed that some carers evidently enjoyed attending sessions and anticipated them as being times for their own recreation. Importantly, too, the leader and the volunteers would take time to listen to the carers, showing an interest in their lives, valuing them for themselves, not just seeing them as supporters.

Some of the churches hosted support groups solely for carers, or otherwise signposted them to local groups run by the Christian agency. It seemed to work better when these met weekly, so that the interval between sessions was not too long if a carer missed a session occasionally. It was clearly difficult for some carers to be able to attend these groups without their relative, who would need support in their absence.

Faith support

For those with a desire for faith input, some of the churches offered mid-week worship services, usually shorter and in a more traditional style. Again, these were not just targeted at people living with dementia but were undoubtedly familiar and appropriate for those who had attended church services prior to developing the condition. The building, symbols, liturgy or familiar format, song choices, and style of worship were all designed to be helpful to those whose longer-term memories would still be strong enough to remember them. This enabled people living with dementia to worship in a form that they might have used all their lives within their familiar church communities.

Leadership and awareness

The most important aspect of provision within these churches, was the leaders' own awareness of the needs of families living with dementia and the desire to support them. Most of the church leaders I spoke to had had some level of training, and Immanuel Church in particular invested in training all its staff, including the leadership, the administration team, and the volunteers.

Advice, signposting, and information

Churches are also suitable and convenient venues for information sessions, during which various professional or charitable organisations can raise awareness of local and national services which may be of help to families living with dementia. These include visits from the local Citizens Advice Bureau, the Red Cross, and GPs, or being used as a vaccination drop-in location. Face-to-face sessions in a familiar and local setting particularly reach those who are unable or uncomfortable with accessing information from other locations or the internet.

While people should be made aware of potential sources of help at the point of diagnosis, this does not always happen, or they find it hard to take in information at the same time as receiving the diagnosis. When I have spoken with family carers whose relative has either deteriorated in health or has died, I have frequently been told: 'I wish I had known about this service before.' Churches can signpost their congregations and communities because of their own knowledge of local services and because of having contact with those who might benefit from this information.

Churches also act as hubs, advertising local events and activities. When I was running community music groups, churches were one of the places I would leave flyers, and they were happy to include an item on their regular newsletters. As families living with dementia have limited outings, churches become one of the few channels through which they get to know what is happening within the local community. If churches are also networking with local agencies, such as GP surgeries, social services, or charities, reciprocal information-sharing can reach more families, and these other bodies may recommend or direct people to church activities through social prescribing.

Dementia information training sessions can reach many who are either living with the condition themselves or are family carers, wider family, friends, or church members. My church has hosted a couple of sessions and also made leaflets and books available. For speakers to come, it makes it worth their time to speak to a large group, so it may be worth inviting other local churches to join.

These sessions appeared to be beneficial to all who attended, but were perhaps especially useful to address wider family and friends who might not have had such understanding or urgency to become informed about dementia. This potentially encourages more involvement from a wider support network around the person living with dementia and their main carer, thereby reducing their isolation. For example, I noticed how church members acquired more confidence in visiting families living with dementia.[1]

More needs to be met

Church leaders I spoke to were all aware that there were still more needs to be met than they were currently doing. One was particularly concerned to change the culture and thinking within her church as regards ministry among older people, particularly those living with dementia. She had noted how, when planning events, there was always a regard for young people and families which was not matched with consideration of the needs of older people or people living with dementia specifically. She felt it would be useful to have a case study of a church event to analyse the impact on those attending.

Familiar forms of worship were the priority for another church leader, who realised that worship services in her church did not have sufficient balance between more contemporary forms and styles and the more traditional. A couple of my interviewees recognised that, as they themselves had aged, the style of worship that they had grown up with became increasingly precious to them, so they could identify with why that would be significant for people living with dementia, whose long-term memories would help to connect them with their past church experience. Styles of music for churches have always been a contentious issue; however, a consideration of all the generations present in a service would help to ensure that nobody was left without a helpful means of expressing their worship.

Another church leader was focused on having the right personnel to facilitate this ministry. She was conscious of the advancing age of those serving older people and was concerned that there would be younger church members to continue the ministry to older people. More than one of these leaders of ministry to seniors felt they were unable to do any more themselves. It was clear that, while they had a passion for their work, this was not shared by many others in their churches. They were conscious that they needed enough support from within their churches to be able to continue such a ministry.

It was noticeable, too, that most of these churches did not feel they had the expertise to deliver support to families living with dementia. It may be a matter of building confidence among churches that it is something they could manage. The only essential requirement is a willingness to learn and to serve these families.

Immanuel Church was also open to learning from research into dementia and what had been found to be helpful to people living with the condition, drawing on this and integrating it into its practice. This learning was applied in the reminiscence sessions, with the use of a wide variety of activities which exercised different skills, and trialling of new ones.

All the churches recognised that they could benefit from further training in how to support people living with dementia. Coupled with this, they wanted closer partnership with organisations who could give the support, resources, and expertise to equip the churches. This might give them the confidence they lacked.

Perhaps the most striking aspiration was to have more people appointed to a specific paid role of ministry to older people. From my own observations, the church having this commitment to the work clearly had an impact on the amount of time and energy given to this ministry, ensuring that the needs of families living with dementia cannot be overlooked. As dementia becomes increasingly prevalent with age, this will be an important consideration for all churches.

So far, I have concentrated on the provision given to families while they are still in attendance at their churches. However, as dementia progresses, the need for support becomes even more necessary, as I will go on to consider.

13

Ministry beyond church attendance

'Don't urge me to leave you or to turn back from you.
Where you go I will go, and where you stay I will stay.'
RUTH 1:16

My research focused on the needs and support of families living with dementia who were still able to get out to events organised by local churches. From my previous experience as a music therapist and current experience as an Anna Chaplain, I am aware of the needs of families beyond the stage of being able to maintain a healthy level of social engagement. So in this chapter, I draw on my personal observations and anecdotal accounts, plus what I have gleaned from various sources while I have been immersed in this subject to consider ways in which church support continues to be required and how it may be offered.

Support at times of transition

There may come a stage in the progression of the dementia when it becomes too difficult to get out to any activities at church – or anywhere else for that matter. Some people, aware of their failing abilities, lose the confidence to engage in pursuits they used to enjoy. A friend explained how her attempts to encourage her husband to engage in any activities beyond the home were met with a negative response. In other cases, the changes in behaviour of their relative makes attending any groups a cause of embarrassment and great anxiety to the family carer. What would have been a simple exercise, like using public transport, eating in a café, or even just getting somebody ready to go out, becomes such a major challenge as to deter both the person living with dementia and their carer from venturing out.

This is the point when the family needs support more than ever. Domiciliary care provided by social services or a local agency is usually to assist with such practical tasks as getting someone up, washed and dressed, and perhaps ensuring they have meals and take their medication. Professional carers are working to tight schedules and budgets and have little time to do more than these practical jobs, so stimulation and social contact are limited.

It is important to affirm family carers in taking time out for respite for the sake of their own health and resilience. Family carers can feel that only they can adequately attend to their relative's needs. One husband who brought his wife to my music group was clearly in severe pain with a hernia, but found it very hard to accept help when someone offered to look after his wife while he had treatment. However, another carer wisely took the opportunity for a fortnight's respite occasionally, ensuring her husband was cared for in a local care home while allowing herself time to enjoy some recreation in order to sustain herself in the caring role. Churches can support carers by helping them to consider alternative courses of action and then encouraging them in taking steps to look after themselves.

However, even with more professional input, the lack of social interaction at this stage may become extreme. A church friend who had always been very sociable and active described how difficult she found it to have only the company of her husband, who in this phase said very little, was not interested in doing anything, and was probably suffering from depression. As was evident through lockdown, isolation has a detrimental effect on someone's cognitive and emotional well-being, thus exacerbating the functional decline for someone living with dementia. For the carer, too, this increases their pressures and stresses, potentially leading to a similarly harmful impact on their own mental health, which in turn can result in a deterioration in the relationship with their relative. Sadly, sometimes there are tensions and resentment around how little of the responsibility of care is shared by other family members. While not getting involved in the family quarrels, churches can at least listen and permit carers to 'offload' their frustration or anger. We should not underestimate how being heard can reduce emotional damage.

If churches have developed a relationship with the family, they can help in several ways at this time of greater isolation.

First, they can make an effort to **keep in contact**, so that the family does not feel abandoned. This might mean making a regular phone call or visit. In my music therapy role, I visited one couple at their home every week, playing music with the husband while his wife seized the opportunity to do some paperwork or a have a quick dash to the shops. A couple from my church appreciated me dropping in to chat; although the husband found speech difficult, he would be present, as his wife and I exchanged bits of news. She valued having contact with the world outside the home, and it may have given a little stimulation to her husband.

Home visits do raise issues of safeguarding: churches should adequately assess risks, have necessary policies in place (including for lone working and risk assessment) and ensure all team members are familiar with them, and take practical measures to ensure the safety of both the family and those visiting. As my musical client's memory deteriorated, he became confused and fixated on doing some things which were no longer realistic or safe, and he began to show some disinhibited behaviours. I was very aware of the safeguarding issues and was about to call an end to my visits, when there was a crisis which precipitated him going into permanent residential care. For all the concerns about safety, however, I would argue strongly that, with proper attention given to managing potential risks, visits should continue and are such a vital support to these families. Alternatively, a regular phone or online call can help to counteract the feelings of isolation.

Another way in which church members may become involved is to **offer practical assistance.** It may be that the person living with dementia used to attend to particular jobs in the home, which now fall on the family carer. An offer to mow the lawn, put up a shelf or do another practical task might really help. One more area in which churches may assist is in offering lifts to appointments. If this is done on the basis of friendship, there will be no need for extra insurance, however it is still wise to check on the details of an insurance policy.

Churches can continue to **offer specifically religious support** for these families, who, though no longer seen, are still part of the community that is served by a local church. After all, churches have a particular responsibility to supply Christian spiritual support. Of course, offering Communion has long been an important way of sustaining people's faith when they can no longer attend their local church. Some churches have continued to provide online services after lockdown ended, and families may need technical assistance to ensure they can avail themselves of these. Receiving church service sheets and newsletters can also help families to feel connected, and it is helpful if paper copies can be available for those who do not use the internet. Supremely, we should continue to pray for these families, so in need of God's help.

Help in times of crisis

Sometimes the next stage for these families begins with a crisis resulting in a hospital admission. This brings new challenges. The person living with dementia may become disorientated in this new environment, and hospital staff may not have the expertise and time to understand and address the issues around dementia, especially if the admission was due to another cause, such as a fracture. Travelling to and from hospital, and the emotional upset of being precipitated into this new situation, takes its own toll on the carer, with increased anxiety about the future beyond the hospital admission. Again, this may be a very lonely experience, so church support can make a real difference. One of the family carers I interviewed saddened me by her account of the experience of being with her husband during hospitalisation. She witnessed other patients being visited by chaplains and leaders from their churches, but she felt that, because she was with him, it was assumed that nobody else from her church needed to visit her husband.

Offering to share hospital visits or accompanying the family carer may ease the pressure on them and give their relative the comfort of seeing another familiar face. Once more, keeping in contact and expressing concern help the carer to feel less alone. A designated person can relay the latest news to others at church, rather than the carer being bombarded by kind enquiries from many well-wishers. When a regular guest at the reminiscence sessions fell and broke her hip, phone calls to her husband from the leader kept the contact until she was well enough to return some months later. Communication during a similar incident with another family meant that the carer and her husband did not feel forgotten and, after rehabilitation, were glad to be able to resume their attendance after many months. In both cases, there was a noticeable deterioration in the cognitive functioning of the person living with dementia, but, because relationships were already well-established, they felt safe to return to the group, where they received a warm welcome.

Beyond living at home

There may come a time, though, when family carers have to admit that they can no longer provide the level of support their relative needs at home. At a particular stage in the development of dementia, care at home can become impossible, due to either physical demands or changes in behaviour. In the case of my musical contact, the need for residential care became evident when, due to his frustrations at being unable to understand realities or communicate effectively, he became violent. Such a story is sadly, not unique, and alerts us to the reality that there may come a point at which professionals need to take over more aspects of a person's care, and a more permanent solution is required.

For some family carers, while acknowledging that residential care has become inevitable, this often remains a difficult and painful decision, which may well engender a sense of guilt or failure at no longer being able to support their relative alone. A Christian friend who had adapted the family home to accommodate and facilitate her mother to live there told me, 'I was the last person to recognise that I could no longer manage.' Churches can be helpful in listening to carers expressing these difficult emotions without judgement and affirming them in their decision.

Helping carers to understand that there can be benefits for both them and their relative may tip the balance of the argument towards taking this step. Family carers, released from the 24-hour support they have been giving, and perhaps from the physically demanding aspects of that task, can enjoy opportunities to resume activities and interests they had prior to the impact of dementia, and hence time visiting their relative in the care home may be relaxed and improve the quality of the relationship. For some people living with dementia, the move into residential or nursing care can be very positive, too, although I am conscious that that is not everyone's experience.

Dementia UK, whose specialist nurses, known as Admiral Nurses, support carers of people living with dementia, has helpful guidance on making this decision and nurses on their helpline can give individual support by phone or video call.[1]

After the move into residential care

Once someone has moved into a care home, there is still an important role for churches to play to ensure that they do not feel severed from their communities or abandoned. One of the anxieties expressed is that this step is an end to someone being part of their community. There is stigma around care homes, as well as dementia, so helping people adjust to this new situation is very important. One of the issues is around the permanence of the change to living in care. Someone told me: 'I am afraid I have come here to die, and I don't like that.' If churches continue to visit and make the person feel they are still remembered by their community, it helps to reduce the feeling of irretrievable disconnection or abandonment. Care homes themselves are increasingly concerned to preserve these community links , offering open days, coffee mornings, or public events. Churches should seize the opportunities to strengthen their connection with both residents and staff.

While help with physical and personal care may be attended to by the move into a care home, the spiritual needs of the person living with dementia may not get the same priority. This is where, for regular church attenders, the link with their church community can so helpfully address these needs. The care home I visit as an Anna Chaplain is really appreciative of my availability to spend time with people who cannot leave their rooms to engage in the programme of activities organised by the home. It also recognises that the staff are busy doing particular tasks, so only have brief opportunities for conversation. Having time for the specific purpose of listening to people is invaluable and is something churches may be able to supply, with suitable training.

For someone with memory loss, the new, unfamiliar environment of a care home can create confusion and the undefined sense that they 'need to go home'. (Thankfully, this is not always the case.) Visits from long-term church friends can potentially relieve this sense of displacement, although care needs to be taken when leaving, so that the lasting memory of the visit does not feel like another abandonment or a disappointed hope that the resident would be leaving together with the visitor. It may spare the person distress to avoid saying 'goodbye', instead just 'popping out to the toilet' or suchlike, to explain your disappearance without emphasising that you are leaving. The book *Contented Dementia* offers a comprehensive strategy of going along with someone's confused beliefs to reduce stress and upset,[2] although some feel that colluding with someone's delusions and effectively lying about reality is dishonest. It is important to balance these concerns with the emotional well-being of the person.

Care homes have standards monitored through inspections which include the requirement to provide support which meets cultural, spiritual, and religious needs. In seeking to be 'person-centred', care homes can work collaboratively with churches and other faith organisations in enabling spiritual and religious needs to be met.

Churches could usefully inform themselves about appropriate ways in which to deliver worship services for those who have dementia. Using traditional forms of liturgy and Bible translations, the Lord's Prayer, and familiar readings, such as Psalm 23, are important for assisting memory, and thereby making the service recognisable and engaging. A member of a former church I attended had a short-term memory of less than one minute, but, as soon as we began the familiar form of the service, she was completely enabled to worship. A friend told me how her mother 'put right' the leader of a service in her care home because he was not using the traditional form of the liturgy! Other considerations include the length of the service, speaking slowly, having large-print service sheets, and acceptance of unusual behaviours.

There are useful resources available for running worship services, from practical guidelines, such as those by Growing Old Gracefully, Shaftesbury, or the Methodist Homes Association, to ready-made orders of service, such as those produced by Spiritual Eldercare.[3] Other practical aids include large print hymn sheets and simple shortened service structures.

In addition to more conventional forms of service, there are other creative ways in which to offer Christian teaching. Truth Be Told is a programme for simple scriptural truths to be shared in an intergenerational service, which encourages families with young children to engage in worship with older people. As it is a multisensory experience, it would be especially appropriate to use with people living with dementia. Based on the principles of Messy Church, Messy Vintage offers a way of being church and engaging in a simple act of Christian worship in hospitable, creative ways. *Celebrating the Seasons in Residential Care Homes: A service for every week of the year* was written by Lindsay Pelloquin and Jaye Keightley, drawing from the ecumenical work of The Gift of Years Rugby, through which Anna Chaplains work in care home teams across Rugby.[4]

One of the challenges I have witnessed of providing worship services in care homes is that of having the space and uninterrupted time in which residents can engage without distractions. The degree to which this is provided varies from home to home. There is not always a physical space, apart from a large lounge in which most residents are seated, often, sadly, with a television on. It is important to agree with the manager the most convenient time and setting for services, to fit in with the home's routines. It may be necessary to stress, maybe on more than one occasion, how important it is to the residents not to have that time interrupted, but also to exercise grace with the care staff who are only trying to do their job. The best example of support I have found in a care home was where staff members were sitting with residents, helping them to find their place in the order of service or in following a hymn. If things are to go well, it means investing time in building relationships with the staff, affirming and appreciating them, often in full-on shifts that are little valued or financially rewarded. It is also good to remember that we go in as visitors, so we have to recognise and cooperate with the priorities and daily routines of the home.

As a practical measure to signal the beginning of the service, it is helpful to play a hymn or familiar chorus. This might assist someone living with dementia in recognising that what is about to follow is a time of worship. Music also provides a helpful cue for the serving of Communion and the end of the service. Other prompts could include arranging a small cloth to indicate the Communion table, a cross and, of course, the chalice and paten. Having these aural and visual cues is important when services are taking place in a room which is not otherwise distinguishable as a place of worship. It is also encouraging if there is a small team who can model the responses or swell the singing, so there is a sense of being in a congregation. Sometimes a resident can assist with taking an active part in an aspect of the service. I have known someone living with dementia who could still accompany the hymns on a keyboard that she had played for years in her church. Others may still be able to read a passage of scripture or even help with serving Communion if they used to do this regularly in the past.

Worship services, though, are only one possible way for churches to keep the relationship live with former church attenders and to show they are not forgotten. These means of connection can take many forms, and fruitful partnerships can involve the whole church through the different gifts and abilities within a fellowship, strengthening the relationship not just with individual residents but with the whole care home. Embracing Age has a whole list of suggestions as to how to do this: giving thank-you gifts to staff, making cards for residents, presenting bouquets of flowers to residents and staff alike on special occasions, producing laminated photographs, offering pastoral visits or involvement in activities, knitting items for residents (Immanuel Church creates delightful 'prayer bears'), donating clothes items such as shoulder capes, or offering IT support to facilitate communication between residents, family, and friends.[5] The beauty of this range of ways of supporting is that it can include church members who might not physically be able to attend the care home but can still be involved in this ministry.

Some care homes display a photograph of the resident at a younger age on the door to their room. Other care homes create a small 'life story' booklet on the admission of a new resident, including such information as their favourite music, preferred clothing, or love of pets. Churches who have known the person well, maybe over many years, could contribute to this account, which not only helps visitors to have talking points, but also gives insights and value to the person in the eyes of the staff, who have only known them in the later stages of dementia.

Some people find visiting someone living with dementia difficult, wondering what to talk about when verbal communication is limited. There are many useful resources available that can assist with engaging people living with dementia. Libraries not only have appealing books of themed reminiscent pictures to prompt conversation, but also artefacts that may trigger memories, such as 45-rpm records, cooking implements, cigarette cards, or tools. The Memory Box Foundation[6] also provides boxes of era-appropriate items which will resonate with the older generation. Knitters or crafters, including children, can make 'twiddlemuffs'[7] or activity boxes to reawaken tactile memories of, for example, handling different fabrics and fastenings or familiar hand tools.

Personalised activities or memorabilia, though, are always the most effective means to stimulate and create connection for people living with dementia. One of my music group members had made a beautiful photo album, not only selecting pictures of significant and precious moments in her father's life, but also writing captions under each one to remind him, and anyone who shared the album with him, of why they were important. He looked at it daily with great enjoyment. Making a personalised playlist – perhaps with the technical assistance of younger people – can also trigger pleasurable memories and can be available after the visit has ended. Jennifer Bute has produced a very helpful flyer, recommending dos and don'ts for visiting someone living with dementia.[8]

Intergenerational involvement can also be a fruitful form of connection and a counter to UK society's increasingly separate activities for different generations. Many Anna Chaplains are involved in projects linking local care homes with children's nurseries, schools, or church toddler groups. An Anna Chaplaincy Easy Guide on linking care homes with local schools shares ideas from Alton in Hampshire, where Anna Chaplaincy first began, and a new Anna Chaplaincy book aimed at care home staff (entitled *Enabling Spiritual Care*) gives suggestions for working with schools and churches to bring children and young people into care homes.[9] In my experience of inviting pre-schoolers into my music sessions, I saw there was an instant rapport with my older participants, and the non-verbal communications between them dispensed with the need for speech. One woman in particular, who had been a mother, instantly beamed as the children entered the room.

Similarly, I have witnessed the enjoyment of residents in a care home at the visit of a dog, with the easily remembered responses of patting or stroking the dog affording an instant rapport. Of course, it is necessary to check with the care home first if this would be welcomed, and the dog would have to be friendly and amenable to being among strangers.

Special times of celebration, such as Easter, Harvest, and Christmas, might afford opportunities to introduce a larger group from a local church, for example, singing carols or presenting harvest donations to the care home. It is also important to offer opportunities for reciprocal giving, allowing people living with dementia an opportunity to be the donors, perhaps of simple crafts that they have made with the home's activity coordinators. This affirms a sense of dignity and signals to others how dementia may not rob people of all their abilities.

The longer I have worked in the field of dementia, the more I have understood the importance of not underestimating or limiting what people might enjoy or can engage in. One care home tapped into the corporate social responsibility of the nearby orchestra, inviting players in to give experiences of playing on musical instruments; I saw a picture in the local paper of a 100-year-old playing the violin. Another care home owned some allotments and took their residents there on warm days to dig, plant, or just sit on a bench watching the others at work, and I have seen waist-high planters in another residential home's garden, facilitating those who still have green fingers. When it was time for the town carnival, a care home teamed up with a local company that hired out bicycles for people with disabilities, enabling the residents to ride in the carnival while the staff did the pedalling!

Churches will have members of all ages with different experience, skills, and interests; if they were to offer these to care homes, it might open up many opportunities for people living with dementia to engage in, support the home in providing meaningful and enriching activities, and all while maintaining the connection with the local community.

One of the ways in which Christians can help change the perceptions of people living with dementia is to pay attention to what individuals are still capable of and to support them in maintaining that ability when possible. I have had the privilege of accompanying people to the end of life by supplying musical opportunities. It appears that the ability to respond to music is one of the last aptitudes to go. So, although someone might be non-verbal and bed-bound, they could still join in on the beat on a drum or time their response to fit at the end of a phrase. In one care home I visited, a resident was encouraged to accompany the maintenance officer on his rounds, which kept alive his interest and enjoyment of practical tasks. When I have been doing music sessions in care homes, the instinct of some residents has been to offer to help issuing song sheets: for those who have had a lifetime of service, this instinct does not disappear when dementia arrives.

Supporting the family carer once the relative has moved into residential care

In many ways, once the relative with dementia has settled into a care home, life is easier for the family carer. They have time to do things which they might have been unable to do for years, and their relationship with their relative may be improved for not feeling exhausted or drained by the level of support they have been giving up to that point. It is easy to assume, though, that once their relative has been accommodated, everything is okay for the carer. However, there may still be a need for church support. For carers as well as their relative, the complete change in their circumstances may require considerable adjustment.

Having been providing 24-hour support, the carer has to adjust to an empty home and a change from routines they may have had for years. Again, this is not always a negative experience, but churches can be there to support them in this time of enormous change. It is likely, too, that this move happens after a period of greater isolation, their social circle may have shrunk, and they may have lost confidence in their ability to circulate and engage in activities. For church attendees, the connection with a fellowship may well have weakened. Churches should be aware of those who have been absent for some time in order to maintain the relationship. Once the relative with dementia has moved into a residential care home, an invitation to meet up with someone may encourage the carer to venture back into society. Sometimes, due to the discomfort felt by church members on witnessing the changes in the person with dementia, both carer and cared-for have been neglected, so there may be some anger and resentment on the part of the carer. This will need careful handling and grace if the relationship is to be restored. Similar to the temptation to avoid someone who has been bereaved, church members might feel uncertain how to talk about the relative with dementia. It would be advisable to ask the carer how they feel and what support they would like.

Once the move has happened, the family carer may continue to feel guilty at not providing care at home, especially if their relative takes time to adjust or is very unhappy. Affirming the wisdom of the decision may help to counteract doubts that this was the right course of action. Carers may also be distressed by the deterioration in their relative. Listening to these painful feelings can provide a release.

Depending on how near the care home is, carers may need lifts to visit their relative. They might appreciate someone else visiting the care home once a week, so that they are satisfied that their relative has received a visit, but are able to take time to relax. They may have financial worries, and big decisions to make regarding their homes, which it helps to voice, and someone without the emotional involvement might be able to assist them in forming a plan or direct them to the right channels to get the advice they need. Of course, it is up to the family carer to decide what help to accept; the important thing is that they are aware that the church is still there for them and that they feel able to ask for help if they want.

End of life and beyond

As the progression of the condition reaches the last stage, there may be many symptoms, including weakness of body, inability to swallow, and lack of speech – although that may have happened much earlier. Even now, if the family desires support, the church still has something to offer. I spent some time in my music therapist role on a dementia unit within a care home. I was able to visit people who were bed-bound and in the last weeks of life. It was a joy to be able to connect with them through music, using songs that were meaningful for them and affording them the possibility of responding on percussion instruments. As Wendy explained in the first part of this book, there are other forms of creative arts that similarly enable the person to communicate and feel connected. For Christians, the singing or playing of a recorded hymn, the reading of scripture, and prayer can be great sources of comfort.

When death occurs, some family carers express the sense that they 'lost' the person that they loved long before, as the dementia wrought such changes in them as to make them unrecognisable. So, for some, grief at this final ending is tempered with relief that that first loss is ended. Friends of mine shared their joy that their dearly loved relative was released from dementia, while experiencing sorrow as they missed him. For others, though, it might be the moment at which the grief they have held on to for so long is finally released. As with any bereavement, the experience of losing someone to dementia will be different for everyone, so it is unhelpful to generalise about how it might affect them. However, the person's death can give the family carer the opportunity to reflect on their relative's life prior to developing dementia, and the relationship they once had with them.

Funerals and memorial services are particularly helpful in providing that long and complete view of someone's life. If the person was a regular member of a fellowship, the whole church can contribute to that portrait, celebrating their contribution. This provides everyone with the opportunity to grieve. One difficulty may be the length of time the person was out of circulation, so not remembered as they were before they had dementia by the current membership. This makes it doubly important to have some form of service to mark the person's death and to remember and celebrate their life. I attended the funeral of someone I had only known in the later stages of dementia. To hear of the amazing things he had done in the past revealed a whole picture of a remarkable man, and enabled me to appreciate and recognise who he was. Whoever leads the funeral or memorial may need to dig a bit deeper to unearth the story of the life of someone who had dementia, but we need to recognise their worth and celebrate their life just as we would with anyone.

Marking someone's death and acknowledging their value is important for other residents and staff in a care home, too. I have seen very different practices in care homes, from coffins being smuggled out under cover of night to residents being invited to stand as a mark of respect as the coffin was carried out. Churches may be able to suggest helpful ways for people to be remembered or to provide memorial services to facilitate the grief of both residents and staff.

After a funeral, whether for someone with dementia or anything else, there is a strange vacuum in which the family member begins to embark on a totally different life. Again, the church can be available to offer support. If the family were involved in church life, it might become the natural place to find relationships. If not, or if it was only the person who had dementia that had the church connection, the relationship could either dwindle or it might be the start of the family carer's search for meaning and engagement. A daughter from one of my groups, whose father had a very active faith, discontinued her relationship with the church after his death, as the association with him felt too painful. In contrast, when I visited a community music group, I was surprised to learn that many of the volunteers had been bereaved; they found the group to be supportive, partly due to sharing memories of their relative and partly as an opportunity to do something positive and meaningful with their new free time. Immanuel Church offers 'After Care', a bereavement support group in which members often become the best sources of support to each other. As in all areas of support, churches need to ask what carers would find helpful.

A continuum of care

As I hope is apparent, churches might accompany families living with dementia throughout the whole journey of the condition, demonstrating love in practical and spiritual ways. However, as I learned during my research, this is not always happening. I will go on to consider some possible reasons for this.

14

What's stopping us?

Then the Lord said to Cain, 'Where is your brother Abel?'
'I don't know,' he replied. 'Am I my brother's keeper?'
GENESIS 4:9

It appears to be unusual for churches to offer targeted support for people living with dementia, and the particular needs of family carers are likewise seldom catered for. There may be several reasons why churches are not reaching out to these families: fear and stigma around the condition; practical difficulties in maintaining contact with these families; lack of confidence in how to support people living with dementia; unawareness of the mutual benefit of inclusion of these families; churches' other priorities; and, sadly, evidence of ageism. There may also be some practical considerations.

Fear of dementia

Dementia is now more feared than cancer by those over 50. I have heard people describe it with such terrifying language as 'a long death' or someone as having become 'an empty shell'. This fear may arise from several causes.

First, it may be due to observable changes in people living with dementia; for example, in their behaviour, their ability to communicate, their short-term memory, or apparent changes in personality. These symptoms may be hardest to accept in a close relative or friend, when they may result in a change in the relationship and the roles within that relationship. For couples, the roles they previously played can completely change, from ones of mutual support to one partner becoming dependent on the other for most aspects of daily life. Once easy-going characters can become very contrary and unobliging, causing their relatives to have frequent quarrels with them over even small issues. It is not surprising that seeing these differences in a close friend or family member engenders fear of the condition.

Noticing these changes in a loved one also confronts us with the reminder of our own vulnerability and mortality. It can feel very uncomfortable to consider that we might succumb to the same condition. A loving daughter, who had shouldered most of the responsibility of her mother's care, told me: 'If I get dementia, shoot me!' While such remarks are shocking, before we jump to criticise, these feelings may have arisen from harrowing experiences and the huge emotional pain of witnessing the effects of dementia in someone well-known and loved.

There is no doubt that the language and portrayal of dementia in the media influences our perceptions of the condition. Or, rather, it is the skewed view of dementia, of only the later symptoms, rather than recognising that it has 'a beginning before the end and so much life to live in between'.[1] Moreover, if we only pay attention to the frightening language around dementia, rather than invest time in the person, we will succumb to a feeling of hopeless paralysis. Accounts of more positive experiences are seldom widely publicised. Nor do we hear much about the earlier stages when people are still able to do some things as well as ever, or of their ability and resourcefulness in compensating for lost skills – or even discovering new creativity.

Another root of fear may be the sense of a lack of control. Despite efforts to find a cure, so far this has only achieved some medication to relieve and delay symptoms in the early stages of some forms of dementia. In the global North we are not good at accepting our limitations, recognising our powerlessness, and experiencing a sense of failure in finding a solution.

The result of these different factors means that there is often avoidance of getting a diagnosis, reluctance in acknowledging that one has dementia, and stigmatisation once that label is given. Some people are in denial about the symptoms they are experiencing, hoping either that they will somehow disappear or that they do not indicate that they have dementia. Those with a diagnosis may be shunned, even by family members or long-term friends who feel unable to face the potential difficulties ahead, leaving both the one with the condition and the immediate family carer even more isolated.

These fears exist within churches as much as in the general population. Some people have been made to feel unwelcome in their churches once they were known to have the condition. A church leader described the negative reaction within a group for seniors in her church when she proposed initiating a ministry to people living with dementia.

We need to be honest about our fears while willing to learn more about the realities of living with dementia, some of which may allay our anxieties and dispel myths surrounding the subject.

Practical difficulties in maintaining contact

Partly due to stigma, people living with dementia may be reluctant to be seen to attend events or activities advertised as suitable for them. Degeneration in cognitive functioning, such as short-term memory loss, sensory distortion, losing the ability to sequence actions, and difficulties in processing speech, can make simple everyday tasks hard to manage. As a consequence of these symptoms, people may become depressed or anxious and have a tendency to withdraw from social situations. Hence, when they most need support, they may not take up what is available. Unusual and unpredictable behaviours may result in carers not feeling confident to bring them along. So, for all these reasons, contact with people living with dementia may be lost.

Family carers, too, may become disconnected for a variety of reasons. They are more inclined to suffer from ill-health themselves as a result of the demands of caregiving. It is also the 'unrelenting demands' of their responsibilities that can leave carers emotionally drained.[2] Moreover, they themselves, not uncommonly aged 70 or more, can have the difficulty of their own disability. They may find it hard to admit how they are struggling to manage. As a result of these factors, they may not have the impetus to find out what support there is or to avail themselves of it. Churches may need to make a greater effort to initiate and maintain contact with such families.

Lack of confidence in ministering to people living with dementia

Many people don't know how to support those living with dementia, feeling less confident in welcoming people with dementia than those with other health conditions. This might be due to a fear that there are too many unknowns about what behaviours might occur, what needs might arise, or how to respond.

This lack of confidence stems from limited awareness about the different forms of dementia and their symptoms and unhelpful generalisations about the progression of the condition. Even in those with the same form of dementia, there may be considerable variation in the way the dementia develops. Psychologist Tom Kitwood recognised that several factors affect someone's well-being apart from the dementia itself: their previous experiences, their relationships, the environment in which they live, and their own personality.[3] So it is unhelpful to assume that the progression of one person's dementia will be the same as another's.

Perhaps there is too much focus on the condition rather than the person. If we are overly concerned about abilities that are lost, we may miss the spirit and character of the person that are still intact. Autobiographies of those living with dementia, like those referred to in the earlier chapters of this book, reveal how, despite some outward behaviours appearing strange and out of character, they are purely symptoms of the condition or attempts to compensate for them. The person remains the same. Psychologist Graham Stokes helpfully identifies how, when traced to their origin, these behaviours make perfect sense.[4]

If we only concentrate on the deficits in functioning caused by dementia, we may see someone as a 'sufferer' and the person then becomes an object of pity, a mere recipient of ministry, or an unfortunate hero. When I began running my community music groups, I was scared of what I might encounter. The joy has been getting to know each different character with their own distinct way of engaging with the music, so I could no more think of them as one type than of any other group of people.

Unawareness of the mutual benefit of including families living with dementia

Some of the language about older people in general, and those living with dementia in particular, suggests that they have nothing to contribute and are merely a drain on resources. Sadly, this can happen in churches, too. But there is another way in which we can view them. God created us to be in community, moreover, to be interdependent. Counter to the prevailing culture in which autonomy and independence are seen as the ideal, we can learn from each other, and be reminded that we are all dependent on both God and other people.

As we were reminded earlier in this book, just because someone may have a diagnosis of dementia, that does not necessarily mean they can do nothing. In a presentation by Jennifer Bute, she described how a church leader assumed she could not give a talk because she had dementia. She has subsequently spoken eloquently on many occasions. A retired vicar recalled the liturgy and actions of taking a Communion service, which he had done many times. It is important to understand what someone can still do well, in which situations they would benefit from support, and which tasks they might be relieved to relinquish. It is well not to assume anything, and whenever possible, to enable someone to continue serving as long as they can.

Family carers might also be viewed as needy, dependent on churches for support while unable to give in return. But those who have experienced the demands of their role are likely to be the best supporters of others in the same situation, able to empathise and relate to other carers in a deeper way than those who have not had that experience. Although their time and energies may be largely taken up with their caring role, they can be an asset to a church, in both this mutual supporting ability, and in modelling and educating church members in how to care for people living with dementia. They may not want their entire identity to be a carer, but may want to maintain other roles within a church.

Those we desire to have in our churches may also indicate how we have absorbed the values of our culture rather than a Christ-like attitude. People with mental illnesses, learning disabilities, and people who are homeless have often positively challenged and disturbed our comfortable congregations. So too with dementia – we would prefer not to have to cope with it. Yet isn't that God's very design for church, that we would have this unlikely fellowship with such a diverse bunch of people in order to demonstrate a different way of relating to each other from that of the world around us?

> *But God chose the foolish things of the world to shame the wise; God chose the weak things of the world to shame the strong. God chose the lowly things of this world and the despised things – and the things that are not – to nullify the things that are, so that no one may boast before him.*
>
> 1 CORINTHIANS 1:27–29

Churches' other priorities

In the course of interviewing church leaders who had a ministry to seniors, I repeatedly heard of the focus on youth and family ministry within their churches. When their own heart was for older people, this struck me as an indication of the prevailing belief in many churches that, unless they reach out to the next generation, they will have no future church. However, if we consider the demographics in the United Kingdom (a population that is ageing and life expectancy increasing), we should, at least in the short-term, be reaching out to the older generation if we want to see our churches full. With the increasing prevalence of dementia, churches also need to prepare for this cohort. Significantly, Immanuel Church has grown most through its ministry to seniors and making every activity dementia-friendly.

In the desire to appeal to younger people, sometimes the style of worship is entirely aimed at that age group. Whatever form of worship is used, there will always be some who find it helpful and others who don't in expressing their praise and feeling nourished in their faith. When a key need for people living with dementia is provision of the familiar, this is a serious concern. Especially for those who may have been part of Christian fellowships for many years, when churches only offer contemporary styles of worship, this may deny them the very means by which they can be sustained and built up in their faith.

The design of buildings is another aspect of churches in which little consideration is given to people living with dementia. One of the churches I studied had had a beautiful new building constructed. However, there were almost no parking spaces, making access extremely difficult for anyone with a physical disability, which would include some people living with dementia. Another church I visited had imaginatively converted another public building for its use, creating a very modern facility shared by other users. However, I had trouble myself locating the reminiscence session held there due to unclear signage, and the black flooring would present challenges to someone with sensory distortion. I have also noticed how churches are increasingly using more contemporary designs of taps and hand dryers in their toilets. If someone's memory is of taps that are twisted on and off and of drying their hands on a towel, using the latest designs of washrooms can be a bewildering experience.

Is there ageism in churches?

I fear that underlying the prioritisation of youth ministry is ageism. Even within churches, there seems to be a view of older people in general as dependent, a burden, and a drain on resources. This is hardly a biblical perspective! Nor is it a fair reflection of the huge number of roles played by the older generation in churches. Giving precedence to the younger generation worryingly suggests that churches have absorbed the value our society attaches to efficiency and productivity.

Jesus himself condemned the neglect of older family members:

> *'Why do you break the command of God for the sake of your tradition? For God said, "Honour your father and mother" and "Anyone who curses their father or mother is to be put to death." But you say that if anyone declares that what might have been used to help their father or mother is "devoted to God," they are not to "honour their father or mother" with it.'*
>
> MATTHEW 15:3–6

He demonstrated his own care in his provision for his mother:

> *When Jesus saw his mother there, and the disciple whom he loved standing near by, he said to her, 'Woman, here is your son,' and to the disciple, 'Here is your mother.' From that time on, this disciple took her into his home.*
>
> JOHN 19:26–27

In a world seemingly obsessed with youth, it can be easy for churches to overlook the gifts, experience, and wisdom of older people. Scripture shows the value God puts on older people: 'Is not wisdom found among the aged? Does not long life bring understanding?' (Job 12:12) We are exhorted to adopt a positive regard for older people: 'Stand up in the presence of the aged, show respect for the elderly and revere your God' (Leviticus 19:32). The Bible even expresses this very strong condemnation: 'The eye that mocks a father, that scorns an aged mother, will be pecked out by the ravens of the valley, will be eaten by the vultures!' (Proverbs 30:17).

The Bible depicts local churches as places where members of all ages have their role to play (Acts 2:17; 1 Timothy 5:1–4; Titus 2). This should be put into practice in the way we support each other: 'Encourage one another and build each other up, just as in fact you are doing' (1 Thessalonians 5:11).

While doing my research, I became aware of the dearth of books on the subject of seniors' ministry, let alone ministry to people living with dementia, as opposed to the great number on youth and family work. Similarly, there are many training courses for youth and family workers, but scarce opportunities to train in ministry to older people, and specifically people living with dementia. One exception is an excellent course by BRF Ministries entitled 'The Spiritual Care Series', which looks at spiritual care in later life, covering the experience of dementia. Clergy and lay workers alike have found the course has deepened their understanding of ministry alongside people living with dementia.[5]

It is helpful to reflect on how we regard success in churches. With national statistics indicating a general trend of decline in church attendance, it is tempting to prize churches that buck the trend in terms of numerical growth. A successful church might be perceived as one which has many programmes running, burgeoning youth groups, and regular families attending, a view that perhaps mirrors worldly measures of effectiveness. However, less attention-grabbing, quiet, relationship-building may be equally valuable, both in terms of attracting people to Christ and of nourishing their faith. If, as we would claim to believe, older people are just as precious as the young, and a person living with dementia does not lose their value, we should be intent on welcoming them just as much as children and families.

Practical considerations

If churches should be offering care and support, they need to be aware of whether and how they can supply what is lacking, while recognising their limits when the specialised care for health and practical needs is best met by professionals. Anna Chaplains, of course, meet some practical needs as part of their care for those they visit. Caraway, the home of Anna Chaplaincy in Southampton which serves older people and those living with dementia,[6] partners closely with other agencies supporting this group. Hence, they can direct people to the appropriate sources of help, while maintaining their specific ministry to supply spiritual support.

Some situations, however, call for the expertise of medical professionals, solicitors, financial advisors, and the like. Churches need to be wise in knowing where their boundaries lie, and that can be tricky at times. If a person living with dementia has a supportive family, it is essential that a church communicates well with them, alerting them to concerns and, where appropriate, suggesting possible solutions. However, some people have no family at all, or those they have live at a great distance or, in some cases, family relationships have broken down. In these situations, the church is their closest 'family' but must take care not to overstep its part in giving advice, particularly in financial matters. It is not only necessary to be familiar with safeguarding policies from social services and denominational leadership, but also to see how they can be applied within a local church, striking the balance between protection and being available to offer support.

Pragmatically, it may be a matter of churches being able to muster the necessary personnel that determines if they can offer this support.

Reliance on volunteers, including those from outside the church, also requires clarity regarding the purpose of the work and a robust process for safe recruitment. Similarly, if a church is to cooperate with other local organisations, there needs to be agreement as to the place of faith in any cooperative effort. If secular agencies, such as local government, GP surgeries, and charities, are to promote, fund, or work with churches, they will need to be satisfied that this is not used as a means of proselytising, and a local church needs to win the respect and trust of their community and a reputation for its care.

These many and varied reasons why churches may feel unable to offer support to families living with dementia – and they may be justified in many of these reasons – may explain why more provision is not being offered.

So, how can we do a better job? In the next chapter I will seek to offer some suggestions as to how to improve our ministry to these families.

15 How churches could better support families living with dementia

Whatever you do, work at it with all your heart,
as working for the Lord.
COLOSSIANS 3:23

Changing beliefs and attitudes

Before they undertake any action, churches need to reflect on their beliefs about dementia and their attitudes to people living with this condition. We are so influenced by the negative messages about the condition that we need to step back in order to allow our thinking to be guided by a biblical perspective. As the first part of this book indicates, Christians should allow their beliefs to be challenged, particularly by the lived experiences of those with faith and dementia.

We begin, then, with the humble acknowledgement that we are all recipients of God's love before we can do anything: it is God's regard that attributes worth to people, not any ability.

According to psychologist Tom Kitwood, being a person is a status 'bestowed' by others through relationship.[1] It follows that the identity of people living with dementia can be preserved by those around them. As Christian communities we need to enable people living with dementia to sense God's ongoing personal knowledge of them and to support them in finding ways to express their unique and precious identity as those created in God's image.

However, we also need to be aware that, in the midst of confusion and loss from a terminal diagnosis and progressive symptoms, families, especially those without a Christian faith, may not feel that the idea of being kept (and ultimately restored) by God's remembrance matches their experience, offers them hope in the immediate term, or addresses the all-too-obvious changes due to dementia nor the way in which being human is associated with being 'self-conscious, rational and competent'.[2] Consequently, it might not satisfy the desperate longing for answers to those pressing existential questions.

We may need to 'hold' families, allowing them to come to terms with their losses in their own time, and resist the temptation to give glib and easy assurances, permitting them to express anger or grief as they grapple with the painful realities of their present situation and feared future. In the meantime, the best support may come through practical demonstrations of God's love, as the church embodies the Spirit's life and light. Sometimes a smile, a hug, a beautifully presented afternoon tea, or someone being willing to listen is the most convincing evidence that God has not forgotten those who are struggling to believe.

However, it may be our view of ourselves that needs to change, recognising that we all have limits and are imperfect, vulnerable, and dependent. The very reliance on support of people living with dementia, rather than demeaning a person, can contribute to a healthy awareness of the need we all have for care and dependence. We are well used to thinking of ourselves as people created in God's image, but what if, instead of demonstrating that through our individual lives, we are meant to mirror the relationships within the Trinity? These may be best evidenced by our interdependent relationships and the blessings that come from living and loving together. If we view ourselves from this perspective, we come in humility, regarding people living with dementia as equals, and understanding the necessity of fellowship in facing our struggles.

This view completely alters the balance of our relationships. We need each other, not so that one is unable to contribute anything while the other does it all, but that, in the mutuality of relationships, bearing each other's burdens (see Galatians 6:2), we discover new things about love. We have something precious to learn from having people who are more dependent and unpredictable in our midst. Paul's imagery of the church as a body, particularly his claim that the weakest members are the most necessary (1 Corinthians 12:22), implies a reversal of perceptions of people living with dementia from being a 'burden' to recognising their contribution, and that we have something to receive as well as to give. The slower pace at which people living with dementia can operate requires time and patience, and can serve as a reminder that God's purpose is, as John Swinton reminds us, to have time for each other.[3] I have heard families say that they have learned to appreciate their family member in a new way through spending more time with them and learning to slow down. When we see people living with dementia in this light, it should help us to value their contribution and see the relationship as one of reciprocal blessing.

Our understanding of Christ, as fully human as well as fully divine, may also colour our thinking about dementia. Christ became weak, vulnerable, and subject to suffering. In so doing, he demonstrated his solidarity with humanity, knowing from personal experience exactly what it means to suffer. Churches can point those living with dementia and those struggling with the demands, questions, and heartache arising from their caring role to the one who fully understands. I use the word 'suffer' intentionally, although this is discouraged by some, including the Alzheimer's Society. Their reason, with which I agree, is to encourage people to believe that it is possible to live well with dementia. Nevertheless, receiving a diagnosis and experiencing or observing the symptoms can be deeply troubling. While recognising that people do not want to be defined by their dementia, denying their struggles and avoiding the word 'suffering' may not fairly represent the experience of families living with this condition.

Instead, we may need a different understanding of suffering. If we view the experience of dementia as a potential for re-evaluating the challenges of sickness or adversity, we position ourselves as partners rather than problem-solvers. From this viewpoint, dementia offers an opportunity for reconsidering our response to a person, instead of adopting societal attitudes of fear and disengagement from a disease. It also causes us to admit our powerlessness in the face of suffering.

If God does not value people living with dementia any less for having cognitive impairment, then neither should we. If we alter our perception, we will be able to acknowledge and recognise their contribution, their efforts to compensate for failing abilities, and enjoy a mutually beneficial relationship with them.

If we focus on the deficits in functioning caused by dementia, we may see someone as a victim, a troubling reminder of our own fragility and our powerlessness to find a cure. The person then becomes an object of pity, a mere recipient of ministry, or a heroic sufferer.[4] The parable of the banquet (Luke 14:15–24), implies that in heaven people with disabilities will be welcomed just as they are, not needing to be healed in advance. This viewpoint challenges our thinking about disability.

Jesus' ministry on earth combined justice and compassion. He reached out to individuals whom society had shunned or excluded, upholding them in the face of disparagement, and often reintegrating them within their communities. In reaching out to those whom others neglected, he restored them in body and mind but also in their standing as people of value. As followers of Jesus, we are called to look out for those on the edge of society and to seek to restore them to fellowship. This is not purely an act of compassion; it is also a matter of justice.

Inclusion may not go far enough. It reinforces the sense of those without disabilities being 'doers' and defines people with disabilities as recipients. Instead, the church can offer friendship, a relationship of choice which mirrors the welcome we have all received from God. One carer I interviewed illustrated this well: 'They always talked to him, came over and had a word with him... didn't bypass him because he had dementia.' In Jesus' healing of people who were sick and disabled, there was an additional blessing of them being reintegrated into society. Churches could combat the segregation of people living with dementia, and, like Jesus, get 'close enough to touch'[5] those whom society would shun.

This could, in turn, bring about changed attitudes and engagement in local communities, and challenge the stereotypes and emotive language around dementia.

What we believe about dementia affects our responses towards people living with the condition. As our thinking undergoes a shift to a more scripturally based position, we must allow this to challenge our sense of responsibility towards these families, to look for the person rather than the damage wrought by the condition, and to consider how we can share the journey with both them and their family carer.

Welcome, inclusion, accessibility, and opportunity

Our welcome should be realised in the provision of accessible and appropriate activities, whether worship services and other specifically Christian events or social occasions. This might not require new events, nor do they necessarily have to be specifically aimed at people living with dementia, but sufficient thought and attention must be given to how existing activities can be made dementia-friendly. Such consideration and revision can open up many occasions for the inclusion of people living with dementia, with the added bonus of keeping them socially integrated within their communities.

Becoming dementia-friendly is simply acquiring a basic knowledge of dementia and how to offer support. This enables a whole church to be aware of manifestations of this condition, and to know how to respond. If a whole church is thus equipped, it means that every aspect of church life can be accessible and safe, welcoming, and inclusive.

If possible, carer support groups can be established to enable them to share some of the struggles they are having in a safe space. Caraway, the Southampton-based chaplaincy for older people, including those living with dementia, together with Emotional Logic, has designed a carers' course with the joint aims of giving information about dementia in the early stages and connecting carers with each other from the beginning of their caring role. This seems an excellent model for churches to follow, in that it puts in place the support network which will serve families throughout the progression of dementia. Another course, 'Caring for caregivers and building support teams', seeks to develop churches' awareness of carers' needs and encourage them to consider ways in which to provide appropriate support.[6]

For some carers, being free to attend support groups without their relative is an impossibility. One solution could be for such groups to be run simultaneously with the activity for those living with dementia, thus enabling the carer to attend without being anxious for the safety of their relative but being close to hand if needed. This would require more personnel, but it would be a practical solution. Alternatively, churches can offer carers some respite from their demanding role, even if only for a couple of hours, while their relative attends an event.

Carers can also be encouraged and affirmed in the way churches check on them, listen to their struggles, and take an interest in their own distinct needs. Sometimes simply giving them the opportunity to offload can act as a 'safety valve' to protect their mental well-being.

This requires attentiveness to their absences, too, and follow up to update on changing situations or pressures.

Better understanding and training

An essential task for churches is to become better informed about dementia, not just understanding its different forms and symptoms, but also increasing their awareness of additional issues facing families living with dementia.

It is certainly helpful to have some knowledge about dementia itself. There are many books and online resources, produced by such organisations as Alzheimer's Society and Age UK, which give information about the different forms of the condition.[7] These can help in identifying the particular features and resulting problems that each type presents. Beyond an awareness of the well-known symptoms, such as short-term memory loss, churches may not be alert to other possible features, like perceptual distortion, hallucinations, or the inability to sequence the actions in a common task. Having a basic understanding can help churches to identify the specific difficulties someone may be struggling with. However, it is also vital to recognise that how dementia, even the same type, affects one individual, will not be the same for everyone. Most important is looking for the signs of the unique person that God designed, which remains intact.

In addition to secular organisations, some denominations offer resources and training, such as the Salvation Army and Methodist Church. There are Christian charities, too, that produce helpful information. The advantage of sourcing information from Christian agencies is that their teaching includes a spiritual aspect and balances facts about the condition with hope.[8]

There are encouraging signs that some denominations are seeing the need to promote Anna Chaplaincy, with some becoming specialists in ministry to those living with dementia. Dialogue between local churches and national and regional denominational levels is helping to increase the number and spread of this ministry.

Personal accounts of what it is like to live with dementia can give us very useful insights. Jennifer Bute's most helpful blog, **gloriousopportunity.org**, mentioned in chapter 1, on which she shares from her perspectives as a GP, carer, and now her own first-hand experience, reveals the daily obstacles she faces while living with dementia, and how others can assist in overcoming them. As she does this from the viewpoint of her vibrant Christian faith, it also offers hope and spiritual support. Her blog includes short videos and downloadable leaflets on practical matters, such as what do when visiting someone with dementia or how to respond if they have a 'meltdown'. Similarly, Christine Bryden's second book, *Dancing with Dementia*, provides practical advice about what she, as someone living with dementia, finds helpful (or not!) in others' responses to her needs.[9] Although without the Christian perspective, Wendy Mitchell also offers useful guidance gleaned from her own and others' experiences in *What I Wish People Knew About Dementia*.[10] If we are committed to trying to support people living with dementia, we need to invest time in learning what they find helpful.

Other possible pragmatic solutions or supports that churches can implement include a consideration of modifications to their buildings. Shaftesbury (the operating name of Livability) is a charity which gives advice on how to adapt buildings to assist people living with dementia.[11] Some of these alterations are obvious, such as step-free access, clear signage, and adequate lighting; but others are not so obvious, and churches may need some education about things like the need to have toilet doors of a contrasting colour to the door frame and the need to avoid highly patterned carpets. Such attention can make the difference between someone with dementia feeling safe and confident or confused and distressed.

However, physical support does not end with adaptations of the building. It means being alert to the issues around mobility or other physiological issues. Problems with balance, processing perception, or muscle weakness may increase the need for a helping hand or a slower pace in accompanying someone into a church building. Allocated parking spaces or having a church-owned wheelchair are simple measures to assist with access, but so is looking out for the person who is struggling to push the wheelchair. Having a quiet space for people to withdraw to would help if someone becomes anxious or distressed.

As for many older people, hearing and sight deterioration may be issues which compound the difficulties for someone living with dementia. They may additionally suffer from distortion of sensory information, so, consideration of matters such as volume levels or having a loop system, adequate lighting, contrasting backgrounds for text, whether in print or on a screen, may help to address these difficulties. Most of these adjustments would benefit others within churches, not just those living with dementia.

Apart from these pragmatic solutions, churches can be especially good at the relational aspects of caring for people living with dementia, actively looking out for how they can best give support. It amounts to making the right assessment of situations and giving the appropriate response. We need to be alert to behaviours which may indicate confusion, anxiety, or distress, taking the time to consider potential causes, asking if the person needs assistance, or supplying the necessary cues to them. When one of my music group members hesitated to sit down, I indicated the chair with my hand as well as inviting her verbally to sit. Another person, newly arrived in the room stated: 'I want to go home!' This appeared to be more to do with not knowing why she was there than a real desire to leave, and she soon settled after someone sat and chatted with her. Being aware that people may be, as Jennifer Bute beautifully calls it, 'time travelling', helps us to understand why they might be talking about past situations rather than the present moment, and to know when to give additional prompts to aid memory. However, the priority is ensuring that the person feels safe and comfortable rather than insisting that they have 'got it wrong' about the current reality. One woman who had attended the reminiscence sessions every Tuesday for years was adamant she never came to the church on that day of the week – I was happy to be 'corrected'! Giving priority to someone's well-being should enable us to exercise patience, make allowances, and consider what actions could relieve anxiety or confusion.

This sensitivity to the needs of those with dementia needs to extend to embrace carers, too. Because they are, in many cases, trying to stay strong as they support their family member, carers may present a brave face. It can take time and trust before they remove their mask and reveal just what a toll their role takes on them. One family carer voiced the need for church members to 'talk in a bit more depth' to understand the extent of the load the carer may be bearing. Many carers experience a whole range of emotions, including frustration, grief, and guilt. A non-judgemental approach is essential when listening to them, provides them with a healthy release, and affirms them in the enormous task they are undertaking. There may be no one else to listen to them, as they might not want to 'burden' other family members, so just the simple offering of time for them to off-load can be so beneficial. An increasing number of carers are becoming the 'sandwich generation', seeking to support simultaneously their parents, who may have dementia, and their children, and possibly looking after grandchildren as well – it might be that churches can assist with one of these responsibilities in order to relieve the pressure on the carer.

The advantage that churches have over other organisations is that, due to established relationships, they may have a fuller picture of their circumstances and hence know the issues for both those with dementia and their carers. As a result, they can respond more easily to specific circumstances and to the particular needs of each family in any given time. Hence, they can offer support to people who may not yet have a diagnosis, accompanying them through the progression of the condition, not waiting until the symptoms have worsened. The support that churches can provide can extend beyond the short-term interventions of professionals or crisis moments, to provide the continuity of care to support carers in the long-term. This is essential when the caring role may carry on for many years, often becoming increasingly demanding as symptoms worsen. It does require us to work at maintaining relationships, especially when the family living with dementia no longer attends church activities.

The relationship with the whole family creates a greater range of ways of offering support, facilitating the flexibility to cater for the different levels of dependency of those living with dementia. Because individuals' experience of dementia can differ so widely, it means that while some can manage to do many things with only minimal support, others may require their family member to remain with them when attending events. When the relationship is with the family, not just the person with dementia, these decisions can be reached together. This holistic care for the family extends to the possibility of the carer attending alone. One newly widowed carer continued to attend the reminiscence groups for a while, as a place where she felt both she and her late husband were valued. Another carer, whose relative did not enjoy the sessions, came for his own social benefit and stimulation. Running something as simple as a memory café may provide a little time when both family members can be supported together. Some carers, having lost their relative, want to give back after the help they have received and extend support to other families, sometimes discovering this to be a way of processing their grief or finding new purpose. So, a church can respond flexibly to the different circumstances and preferences of each family.

Practicality and realism

For a church to be able to provide support to families living with dementia, having enough personnel is essential, both paid staff and volunteers.

Churches can encourage people they recognise have the skills and heart for this sensitive ministry to see ways in which they can serve, ensuring they are safely recruited and supported in accessing appropriate training. It is helpful if someone oversees recruitment and support of volunteers so that there is a clear mutual understanding of the expectations and requirements of their role, but also ongoing support and a value attached to their willingness to give time and energy.

The lovely thing about voluntary roles is that they can be at the level at which someone feels comfortable. When I sought helpers for my music groups, one of the people who offered to help had a mild learning disability. She was able to assist with handing round refreshments and, because she was less self-conscious when it came to joining in, would get up and dance, which in turn encouraged my groups members to engage actively. On the other end of the spectrum, I have worked with someone who was a former care home manager and two people who used to work in day care centres – they had much more experience than I do in working with people with dementia.

Immanuel Church has a very positive policy of recruiting volunteers from outside the church, recognising the gifts, abilities, and breadth of experience that they bring, as well as their willingness to offer their time. It does not require every member of the team to be a Christian, but that they respect the Christian ethos and know who to refer to with any spiritual questions. This attitude to partnering with non-Christian volunteers fitted within the church's view of its outreach beyond the church.

One solution to the issue of having enough personnel to minister to people living with dementia is to work in partnership with a professional organisation. This has the advantage of having a well-trained leader to direct the activities, while the church can do what it has much experience in: host the events. This preserves the Christian ethos while outsourcing the expertise to run an activity. Again, there needs to be an understanding regarding any faith input.

Another essential is active promotion of the activities that churches offer. From my previous experience as a music therapist, I found families living with dementia extremely difficult to reach due to their isolation and limited excursions into the community. So churches need to be proactive in publicising what they provide, using the places which these families are likely to visit: GP surgeries, chiropodists, opticians, pharmacies, outpatient departments, etc. Sally Nevitt took this a step further, offering a cream tea in a local supported-living home as a means of connecting with local residents. Every church would need to assess the most appropriate ways in which to make these connections with their particular communities. It takes time to build a reputation, and a good name is earned by the quality of the work and the integrity of the church, but, as trust develops, those who attend regularly become the best advocates and promoters.

Many churches lack confidence to offer ministries to families living with dementia. This could be partially addressed by education and training, but also by trialling small projects and learning from them. Nevitt spoke from what she had learned through practical experience: 'It isn't rocket science. It's not difficult. It's not expensive. There are things you can do.' She gave the example of the church's weekly singing session, saying that all that was necessary was someone with enough confidence to lead. The film showings, too, required little staffing. She argued that what families living with dementia need most is social interaction, stimulation, and a safe and welcoming environment – none of them requiring massive costs or highly trained professionals. Churches might need to attempt something in order to grow in their understanding, skills, and confidence. They will need to find the activities that they feel most able to offer, even if only a few. That could be enough to make a difference for families living with dementia to feel supported and cared for.

However, churches may have to acknowledge their limitations as to the level or the length of time they can offer support when including individuals in groups and activities. Either for reasons of declining health or for behaviours that might be hard to manage, people living with dementia may need more support than we can give. There needs to be realism about the point at which a church's role changes and is more about individual pastoral support than inclusion in activity groups. I have found it hard when people I have supported stop attending because it has become too difficult for them to get to sessions or they are too distressed at their failing powers. In those times, I have had to acknowledge that I might have fulfilled my part in supporting them, just one step in their dementia journey, before I hand over to others to continue their care. I have to relinquish the thought that I can meet every need, and humbly admit my limits, dedicating to God the little that I can do. I have found the story of the starfish an enormous help in getting my contribution in perspective. Very briefly, the story describes a boy picking up individual starfish and throwing them back into the sea after a storm had left thousands stranded on the sand. When challenged about the worth of his efforts, he made the pragmatic statement, 'It made a difference to that one!'[12] If we all play our part, however small, in supporting families living with dementia, we can make a difference at some stage in their lives, while trusting God to continue his care through other agencies.

Even with limited resources, there remain ways in which churches can demonstrate concern and provide some level of support once someone has stopped attending. When lockdown brought my community music sessions to an abrupt halt, I was devastated to think that I could no longer offer this support to my group; so I learned how to create YouTube clips of me singing. When the husband of one of my group members told me that his wife had instantly recognised me when she saw the video, I was so glad to feel there was still something I had to offer. There were some positive lessons from the experience of lockdowns during the Covid pandemic, including the benefit of offering online worship services to people who cannot physically attend church, a rediscovery of old forms of communication, such as telephone calls and letters, and the delivery of 'goody bags' of stimulating items. We have such a range of possible ways in which to keep connection with those confined to their homes that, with creative imagination, there are ways to continue to show that we care.

It is sensible for local churches to begin with an audit of the needs and the already established institutions or community opportunities there are for people living with dementia in their parish or locality. Anna Chaplains are used to doing this, and, if a church is blessed to have one, they can helpfully take the lead in exploring the local provision. Forming or regenerating relationships with key people in these local facilities increases the number of opportunities for the church to engage with families living with dementia. While GPs cannot breach their regulations on sharing personal information about their patients, they are keen to find ways in which people living with dementia can be supported within their communities. Finding appropriate social support can relieve the pressures on primary health care, as often the needs are not health issues. In a surgery local to me, there is a designated community support lead, who is happy to refer patients to any suitable activities or events. So, it requires good liaison between churches and other agencies in order to establish what is most needed and how best to provide it.

Other potential points of contact are community centres, libraries, adult education centres, sports clubs, or arts centres. I was given the opportunity to run music sessions for a local Parkinson's support group in an arts centre. I would urge churches to pursue the links and interests that are already held by their members. I have heard of a 'caged cricket' club, a walking group, a pub quiz (yes, even with memory loss, this appealed to some people with dementia!), choirs, or inclusion in a Men's Shed group.[13] Not all of these were run by churches, but I include them here to stimulate imagination as to what a local church might feel comfortable to do, drawing on the gifts, experience, and passions of their members.

When I joined an online course about the use of creative arts with people living with dementia, it highlighted for me how, despite cognitive decline, people can not only retain creative ability, but even discover new talents. A church friend who started attending an art class produced beautiful watercolour paintings. Once more we need to remember that, just as we all have different tastes and abilities, people living with dementia are just as diverse, so we need to connect with a variety of places where they may have been actively involved for years and be open-minded as to what might appeal to most to them.

However, I would emphasise the invisibility of these families. The ones most in need of support will be those still living at home and no longer engaged in community activities, and therefore, not to be found in a defined location. There needs to be a more determined effort to reach out to them than for other more mobile and integrated members of the community.

Although I have mainly discussed older people, dementia can affect anybody, even those under 50, so we also need to be alert to the fact that those with early onset dementia may not be found in the same places as the older generation. A former work colleague contacted me as her husband, only in his early 50s, had begun to develop symptoms. She was desperate to find some suitable activities for her husband; everything that she had so far discovered was aimed at people at least 20 years his senior. This is a real cause for concern. There may be additional issues for carers of these younger people, too, for example around working, income, pensions, and entitlement to benefits.

Commitment and finance

As the proportion of the population that is over 65 grows, with life expectancy increasing, and with it the incidence of dementia, churches should do more to prepare for this cohort, demonstrating the worth they attach to people living with dementia in the way in which they offer time and money to their care.

If a church is serious about supporting families living with dementia, one way to reflect its commitment is by employing dedicated leaders. These appointments would ensure the prioritisation of this ministry and be key in initiating and adequately resourcing this work. A leader with the passion and commitment to this ministry can inspire and direct a team and raise awareness and understanding in the congregation and in the local community.

The support of a whole fellowship

For this ministry to flourish, though, it also needs the support of the whole local church behind it in willingness to give time, space, service, and prayer support.

This commitment needs to permeate planning, so that there is a conscious consideration that the activities offered by a church are accessible to people living with dementia and that there is a sensitisation of everyone within the church to their needs. The result is an ethos that pervades the whole church, from the patience shown to visitors to the café, the willingness of all staff to jump to the aid of someone who is confused, and the whole sense of welcome from the church.

But it is too easy to assume that, because someone has short-term memory loss or other symptoms, they have lost every ability. People living with dementia may still be able to perform tasks, particularly ones they have carried out for years. Jennifer Bute's eloquence, despite having lived with dementia for many years, has much to teach us. It is important not to make assumptions, but to recognise what an individual might still be able to do. At the same time, it may be stressful for someone to continue their role as they are aware of new difficulties in performing their tasks. It requires great sensitivity to ascertain what someone may feel able to do, or to know what additional help might enable them to continue in their role.

If we are only taking into account their cognitive ability, we are missing other important facets of them as unique people created by God, such as their character, their consideration of others, their dexterity, or their sense of humour. One woman would always crack a joke with her neighbours as she joined the table in the reminiscence sessions. A man who came to my music groups would raise his cap to me, a lovely gesture that he would do almost by reflex. We need to appreciate other aspects of people than just their abilities.

Church members can work together to encourage and bless people living with dementia, as well as being blessed by them, recognising their abilities and helping them avoid loneliness and isolation. The image of Psalm 92 could be applied to people living with dementia as much as any other older people:

The righteous will flourish like a palm tree,
they will grow like a cedar of Lebanon;
planted in the house of the Lord,
they will flourish in the courts of our God.
They will still bear fruit in old age,
they will stay fresh and green.
PSALM 92:12–14

Demonstrating love

The very pinnacle of this practical, interrelational functioning of a church is love. Without being specialists, churches can make such a difference by showing practical care, acceptance, and commitment to these families. Even if there are no specific activities or any targeted support for people living with dementia, love makes a difference to them and their family carers. This loving care can be manifested in a readiness to act, an openness of mind, and a concern for this group that ensures they are provided for. What people often most need is simple: the opportunity to meet in a safe environment, to get out from their homes where possible, to have some stimulation – to feel loved. Without being experts, churches can improve the experience of families living with dementia.

Instilling hope

Ultimately, we are directing people, through our loving presence, towards a relationship with God himself, which alone can offer the hope and strength to sustain families living with dementia.

When we realise the value that God puts on every life, we have reasons to remain hopeful. God's love for us began when he chose us 'before the creation of the world' (Ephesians 1:4), continued when we were 'knit together' in our mother's womb (Psalm 139:13), has remained unwavering throughout our whole lives (Psalm 37:25), is promised to the end of our days on earth (Psalm 23:6a), and keeps us in his everlasting love (Psalm 23:6b). So often the Bible encourages us to take stock of what God has already done in our lives to encourage us to trust him for the future.

The promise of Romans 8:39 that nothing can separate us from God's love in Christ must include dementia, so this gives a real hope to those who know and are known by him. We should pray for those who already have this personal relationship, that they continue to have a sense of his presence, which is possible even with declining cognition, as personal testimonies confirm.

So, in all these various ways, and no doubt others which I have not thought of, we can offer the support, encouragement, and hope that families living with dementia need in the immediate and long-term.

Conclusion

There is hope

> *This hope will not disappoint us, because God's love has been poured out in our hearts through the Holy Spirit who was given to us.*
> ROMANS 5:5 (CSB)

In writing this book we have been conscious of the fact that living with dementia, whether personally or as a family carer, is not easy, and we do not want to deny or gloss over the very real challenges it presents. Neither do we feel ourselves to be experts: it is you who live with dementia and you who seek to support your family members who fully understand the extent of the struggles that dementia brings. We can only seek to learn from what you tell us and our own observations. So, we offer you our contribution with humility, and ask you to forgive us if you do not feel we have adequately represented you.

Our desire is to introduce hope into the picture. Both within individual family circumstances and in church contexts, we want to challenge the predominately gloomy narrative about living with dementia, pointing to examples of positive experiences and recognising the possibilities of ways to support both the person living with dementia and their family carer to experience light in the darkness.

Both of us have had the privilege of having direct contact with some of the pioneers in this campaign to change belief about dementia, whose lives and contribution we find so inspiring. Such testimonies of determination and persistence blow apart stereotypes and entirely negative prognoses, without denying the difficulties of living with dementia. Their accounts testify to the very real possibility of finding hope in the middle of the challenges, and encourage and inspire those of us who seek to follow behind in the battle to change thinking about dementia.

But there is work for us to do to overcome the stigma and fears around this condition. It takes time to shift long-held beliefs when we are constantly exposed to a message contrary to our hope-infused view. Paul exhorts us to 'be transformed by the renewing of your mind' (Romans 12:2). We need to nourish ourselves constantly on stories of positive experiences of living with dementia while deconstructing the stereotypes and myths about the dementia journey. We also need to be willing to rethink our beliefs about what it means to be a person in the light of scripture, revelling in the value that God has given to each one of us. Once assured of God's faithfulness and commitment to our care, we are in a position to explain the basis of our hope to others, if invited, recognising that some may not yet be ready to listen while they are coming to terms with a diagnosis and altered future prospects.

Our greatest hope, though, comes from the character of God himself, the compassionate and just God who has a special regard for the marginalised. His guaranteed promises to supply the grace we need for every trial, of his faithful commitment to care for us to the end of our lives, and that he will never leave us or let us down, shine light into the darkest of situations.

This book is focused on enabling and sustaining a relationship with the living God, with all that implies for our spiritual well-being. It is this relationship that gives us life, strength, and even joy, no matter what we face. As the letter to Romans puts it: 'May the God of hope fill you with all joy and peace as you trust in him, so that you may overflow with hope by the power of the Holy Spirit' (Romans 15:13). Through this relationship we have a hope for ourselves and to offer to our neighbours who may yet have to discover the source of our hope.

None of us are promised a trouble-free life on earth, whether or not we live with dementia, but our hope extends beyond our earthly lives, and Paul reminds us: 'If only for this life we have hope in Christ, we are of all people most to be pitied' (1 Corinthians 15:19). We are assured that, in the span of eternity, our struggles of today will be far outweighed by the glory to come. In the meantime, while we wait, we lean into this very real hope for ourselves and seek to hold it out to all who struggle with dementia.

Our desire is that this book encourages you, causes you to think (and perhaps rethink) what you believe about dementia, and perhaps presents a gentle challenge to you to respond differently. But, most of all, we pray that it will give you renewed hope and courage to persevere.

Wait with hope for the Lord.
Be strong, and let your heart be courageous.
Yes, wait with hope for the Lord.
PSALM 27:14 (GW)

Acknowledgements

Unless otherwise stated, scripture quotations are taken from the Holy Bible, New International Version Anglicised Copyright © 1979, 1984, 2011 Biblica. Used by permission of Hodder & Stoughton Ltd, an Hachette UK company. All rights reserved. 'NIV' is a registered trademark of International Bible Society. UK trademark number 1448790. Scripture quotations marked with the following abbreviations are taken from the version shown. NRSV: the New Revised Standard Version Updated Edition. Copyright © 2021 National Council of Churches of Christ in the United States of America. Used by permission. All rights reserved worldwide. MSG: *The Message*, copyright © 1993, 2002, 2018 by Eugene H. Peterson. Used by permission of NavPress. All rights reserved. Represented by Tyndale House Publishers, Inc. ESV: The ESV® Bible (The Holy Bible, English Standard Version®), © 2001 by Crossway, a publishing ministry of Good News Publishers. Used by permission. All rights reserved. CSB: The Christian Standard Bible. Copyright © 2017 by Holman Bible Publishers. Used by permission. Christian Standard Bible®, and CSB® are federally registered trademarks of Holman Bible Publishers, all rights reserved. GW: GOD'S WORD®. © 1995, 2003, 2013, 2014, 2019, 2020 by God's Word to the Nations Mission Society. Used by permission.

The quotation on pages 52–54 is taken from **memorybridge.org** © 2004–2021, Memory Bridge. All rights reserved.

'King or Queen' (p. 70) published with kind acknowledgement to Living Words Arts, reg charity 1157780 / **livingwords.org.uk**. 'King or Queen', *The Things Between Us* (Living Words Arts, 2014).

The poem on page 71 is taken from *Dementia Positive*. © John Killick. Reproduced with permission of Luath Press Limited through PLSclear.

Wendy Gleadle

My thanks to the following for their interest, support and encouragement.

The Revd Professor John Swinton, chair in divinity and religious studies at the University of Aberdeen and author of *Dementia: Living in the memories of God* and many other titles. I am privileged for his insights and encouragement and permission to quote from our conversations. Frances and I are indebted to him for writing the foreword to this book.

Christine Bryden, author of *Dancing with Dementia*, *Will I Still Be Me?*, and *Letter to the Church*. She has been my true inspiration and I am honoured to have her endorsement.

Dr Jennifer Bute, author of *Dementia from the Inside* and creator of **gloriousopportunity.org**. It was a joy to meet her and a privilege to have her endorsement.

The Revd Robin Thomson, author of *Living with Dementia* and *Unfailing Love* and leader of my online dementia support group. I am grateful for his friendship and encouragement, and for endorsing this book.

Louise Morse, The Pilgrims' Friend Society, and author of *Dementia: Pathways to Hope* and other titles on dementia. I was honoured to have her advice and involvement.

Miriam Banes, The Pilgrims' Friend Society. Miriam kindly wrote an endorsement on their behalf when illness prevented Louise Morse from doing so.

The Revd Tina English, founder of Embracing Age and author of *A Great Place to Grow Old*. I'm delighted by her involvement and her endorsement.

Julia Burton-Jones, Anna Chaplaincy training and development lead. Thanking her for her loving support throughout my Anna Chaplaincy, and for her endorsement.

Debbie Ducille, ministry lead, Anna Chaplaincy for Older People. I am grateful for her encouragement and her endorsement.

The Revd Chris Duffett, artist and creative evangelist, author of *Big Hearted* and *Philip*. I am grateful for his loving support and honoured by his endorsement.

The Revd Glyn Jones, church planter and lecturer in missiology, author of *The Peg and the Pumice Stone*, and my personal tutor when writing my BA dissertation. I am delighted to have his endorsement.

The Revd Canon Brian Dunlop, chair of CaBiC (Cheltenham and Bishop's Cleeve Anna Chaplaincy for Older People) and member of my online dementia support group. I am grateful for his endorsement.

Anna Chaplains, Anna Friends, carers, and dementia support group members: I am indebted to all who sent me personal accounts of how those living with advanced dementia can still experience God.

Louise Voss, former well-being coordinator at Mill House Care Home, and the staff and residents from 2017 to 2024, who were my inspiration and without whom this book would never have been written.

Frances Attwood

I have learned so much from, and been inspired and encouraged by the following:

Dr Jennifer Bute, who not only gave me insights into the experience of living with dementia but radiates her own hope and vibrant faith.

Dr Abigail Maguire, director of learning and student experience at Moorlands College, Dorset. I am so grateful for her belief in my having something useful to say, and her encouragement to publish some of my research findings.

Sally Nevitt, former older people's director, Immanuel Church, Southbourne. She was my first source of inspiration by her comprehensive ministry and commitment to seniors in her church and the local community.

Canon Revd Dr Erica Roberts, former city chaplain for older people, Southampton, and founder of Caraway. Caraway seems to me to offer such an excellent model for encouraging, developing, and supporting churches in ministry to seniors.

Tess Champion, Bournemouth manager, Prama Life, Dorset. She gave me insights into the bigger picture of what churches are offering families living with dementia.

Gay Francia, **Jane Alton**, **Rebecca Osbourne**, and **Tona Carr**, who were all willing to share their experiences of ministry within their churches to families living with dementia.

All the guests and carers who have attended Memory Lane, and from whom I have learnt most about what is needed and valued in church support.

Recommended reading and resources

Océane Agli, Nathalie Bailly, Claude Ferrand, 'Spirituality and religion in older adults with dementia: a systematic review', *International Psychogeriatrics*, 27.5 (2015), pp. 715–25.

Trevor Adams, *Developing Dementia-friendly Churches* (Grove Books, 2018).

Rebecca Atkinson and Ming-Hung Hsu, 'Music has a profound affect on people with dementia', ScienceAlert, 16 October 2024, **sciencealert.com/music-has-a-profound-effect-on-people-with-dementia**

Robert Atwell, Joanna Collicutt, Julia Burton-Jones, David Richardson, Sue Moore, and Matthew Salisbury, *God in Fragments: Worshipping with those living with dementia* (Church House Publishing, 2020).

Rosie Barker, *Six Key Steps to Making a Dementia Friendly Church* (Pilgrims' Friend Society, 2014).

Deborah Barr, *Grace for the Unexpected Journey: A 60-day devotional for Alzheimer's and other dementia caregivers* (Moody Publishers, 2018).

Herman Bavinck, *Essays on Religion, Science and Society* (Baker Academic, 2013).

Richard Behers, *Spiritual Care for People Living with Dementia Using Multisensory Interventions: A practical guide for chaplains* (Jessica Kingsley, 2018).

Diane Bentley, *Lost in Time: God's grace in the midst of dementia* (Trilogy Christian Publishers, 2020).
Dietrich Bonhoeffer, *Christ the Center*, trans. J. Bowden (Harper and Row, 1978).
Maria Bons-Storm, 'Where is God when dementia sneaks into our house? Practical theology and the partners of dementia patients', *HTS Teologiese Studies* 72.4 (2016), pp. 1–8.
Elisa Bosley, Spiritual Eldercare website, **spiritualeldercare.com**
Jane Brotchie, *Caring for Someone with Dementia* (Age Concern, 2003).
Christine Bryden, *Dancing with Dementia: My story of living positively with dementia* (Jessica Kingsley, 2005).
Christine Bryden, 'A spiritual journey into the I-Thou relationship: a personal reflection on living with dementia', *Journal of Religion, Spirituality and Aging*, 28.1–2 (2016), pp. 7–14.
Christine Bryden, *Will I Still Be Me? Finding a continuing sense of self in the lived experience of dementia* (Jessica Kingsley, 2018).
Christine Bryden, 'Letter to the church', *Journal of Disability and Religion*, 22.1 (2018), pp. 96–106.
Christine Bryden and Elizabeth MacKinlay, 'Dementia – A spiritual journey towards the divine: a personal view of dementia', *Journal of Religious Gerontology*, 13.3–4 (2003), pp. 69–75.
Jennifer Bute with Louise Morse, *Dementia from the Inside: A doctor's personal journey of hope* (SPCK, 2018).
Jennifer Bute's website: **gloriousopportunity.org**.
Kenneth Lee Carder, *Ministry with the Forgotten: Dementia through a spiritual lens* (Abingdon Press, 2019).
Tim Chester, *Good News to the Poor: Social involvement and the gospel* (Crossway, 2013).
Joanna Collicutt, *Thinking of You: A resource for the spiritual care of people with dementia* (BRF Ministries, 2017).
Robert Davis, *My Journey into Alzheimer's Disease* (Tyndale House Publishers, 1989).
John Dunlop, *Finding Grace in the Face of Dementia* (Crossway, 2017).
Tina English, *A Great Place to Grow Old: Fresh perspectives on ministry among older people* (Darton, Longman and Todd, 2021).

Wayne A. Ewing, *In the Land of Forgetfulness: Meditations on dementia care as spiritual formation* (Wipf and Stock, 2024).
Kathy Fogg Berry, When Words Fail: Practical ministry to people with dementia and their caregivers (Kregel Ministry, 2018).
Tali Folkins, 'Tips for making your church dementia-friendly', *Anglican Journal* 144.3 (2018), p. 7.
R.T. France, *Tyndale New Testament Commentaries: Matthew* (Intervarsity Press, 2008).
Makoto Fujimura, *Art and Faith: A theology of making* (Yale University Press, 2021).
Caroline George, *Living Liturgies: Transition time resources for services, prayer and conversation with older people* (BRF, 2015).
Rosalie Hudson, 'Disabled or enabled: ethical and theological issues for dementia care', in Elizabeth MacKinlay (ed.), *Ageing, Disability, and Spirituality: Addressing the challenge of disability in later life* (Jessica Kingsley, 2008), pp. 81–93.
Janet Jacob, *Visiting People with Dementia: Principles drawn from experience* (The Pilgrims' Friend Society, 2014).
Oliver James, *Contented Dementia: 24-hour wraparound care for lifelong well-being* (Vermilion, 2009).
Peter Kevern, *Touching God: Dementia and the bodies of Christ*, (WIPF and Stock, 2025).
Peter Kevern, 'What sort of a God is to be found in dementia: a survey of theological responses and an agenda for their development', *Theology* 113.873 (2010), pp. 174–82.
John Killick and Claire Craig, *Creativity and Communication in Persons with Dementia: A practical guide* (Jessica Kingsley, 2012).
John Killick, *Dementia Positive* (Luath Press, 2013).
Michael Kinsley, *Old Age: A beginner's guide* (Rider, 2017).
Tom Kitwood, 'Towards the reconstruction of an organic mental disorder', in Alan Radley (ed.), *Worlds of Illness: Biographical and cultural perspectives on health and disease* (Routledge, 1993), pp. 143–60.
Tom Kitwood, *Dementia Reconsidered: The person comes first* (Open University, 1997).
Ian Knox, *Finishing Well: A God's-eye view of ageing* (SPCK, 2020).

Lee-Fay Low, *Live and Laugh with Dementia: The essential guide to maximizing quality of life* (Exisle Publishing, 2014).
Elizabeth MacKinlay (ed.), *Ageing, Disability and Spirituality: Addressing the challenge of disability in later life* (Jessica Kingsley, 2008).
Elizabeth MacKinlay, *The Spiritual Dimension of Ageing*, second edition (Jessica Kingsley, 2017).
George A. Mashour et al., 'Paradoxical lucidity: a potential paradigm shift for the neurobiology and treatment of severe dementias', *Alzheimer's and Dementia*, 15.8 (2019), p. 1107–14.
Memory Bridge (founded by Michael Verde), **memorybridge.org**
Wendy Mitchell, *Somebody I Used to Know* (Bloomsbury, 2018).
Wendy Mitchell, *What I Wish People Knew about Dementia: From someone who knows* (Bloomsbury, 2022).
Steve Morris, *Memory Café: How to engage with memory loss and build community* (Grove Books, 2017).
Louise Morse, 'Putting the pieces together: dementia information pack', Pilgrims' Friend Society, 2021, **pilgrimsfriend.org.uk/resources/dementia-information-pack**
Louise Morse (ed.), *Worshipping with Dementia: Meditations, scriptures and prayers for sufferers and carers* (Monarch Books, 2010).
Louise Morse, *Dementia: Pathways to hope* (Monarch Books, 2015).
Henri Nouwen, *The Road to Peace: Writings on peace and justice* (Orbis Books, 1998).
Henri Nouwen, 'Community makes God visible', 26 November 2020.
Robyn Plunkett and Peter Chen, 'Supporting healthy dementia culture: an exploratory study of the church', *Journal of Religious Health*, 55.6 (2016), pp. 1917–28.
David Richardson, 'Dementia-friendly churches', in Robert Atwell et al., *God in Fragments: Worshipping with those living with dementia* (Church House Publishing, 2020), pp. 86–110.
Fay Sampson, *Prayers for Dementia: And how to live well with it* (Darton, Longman and Todd, 2017).
Gerda Saunders, *Memory's Last Breath: Field notes on my dementia* (Hachette, 2017).

Dorothy L. Sayers, *The Mind of the Maker* (HarperCollins, 1968).
Shaftesbury, 'My faith matters: a resource to support the spiritual journey of people living with dementia', **shaftesburygroup.org/download/my-faith-matters**
Shaftesbury, 'Travelling together: dementia inclusive church guide', **shaftesburygroup.org/download/travelling-together**
Peter Singer, *Practical Ethics*, second edition (Cambridge University Press, 1993).
James K.A. Smith, *Desiring the Kingdom: Worship, worldview, and cultural formation* (Baker Academic, 2009).
Graham Stokes, *And Still the Music Plays: Stories of people with dementia* (Hawker Publications, 2008).
John Swinton, *Becoming Friends of Time: Disability, timefullness, and gentle discipleship* (Baylor University Press, 2016).
John Swinton, *Dementia: Living in the memories of God* (SCM Press, 2012).
John Swinton, *Raging with Compassion: Pastoral responses to the problem of evil* (SCM Press, 2018).
John Swinton, 'Remembering the person: theological reflections on God, personhood and dementia', in Elizabeth MacKinlay (ed.), *Ageing, Disability and Spirituality: Addressing the challenge of disability in later life* (Jessica Kingsley, 2008), pp. 22–35.
John Swinton, 'What the body remembers: theological reflections on dementia', *Journal of Religion, Spirituality and Aging*, 26:2–3 (2014), pp. 160–72.
Robin Thomson, *Living with Alzheimer's: A love story* (Instant Apostle, 2020).
Robin Thomson, *Unfailing Love: 30 devotions to encourage dementia caregivers* (The Good Book Company, 2025).
Lucy Whitman (ed.), *Telling Tales about Dementia: Experiences of caring* (Jessica Kingsley, 2010).
'Tricia Williams, *God's Not Forgotten Me: Experiencing faith in dementia* (Cascade Books, 2022).
'Tricia Williams, 'What happens to faith when Christians get dementia?', 23 October 2019, **faithinlaterlife.org/news-blog-what-happens-to-faith-when-christians-get-dementia**

James Woodward, *Valuing Age: Pastoral ministry with older people* (SPCK, 2008).
World Health Organization, 'Dementia', fact sheet, 31 March 2025. **who.int/news-room/fact-sheets/detail/dementia**
James Woodward, *Between Remembering and Forgetting: The spiritual dimensions of dementia* (Mowbray, 2010).
Mark Wormell, *Coming to Christ in Dementia* (Mountain Street Media, 2016).
John Zeisel, *I'm Still Here: Creating a better life for a loved one living with Alzheimer's* (Piatkus, 2011).

Information about dementia

Alzheimer's Association **alzheimers.org.uk**
Age UK **ageuk.org.uk**
Carers UK **carersuk.org**
Dementia UK **dementiauk.org**
Glorious Opportunity **gloriousopportunity.org**

Practical resources

Church of Scotland **churchofscotland.org.uk**
Shaftesbury **shaftesburygroup.org**
Methodist Church **methodist.org.uk**
Pilgrims' Friend Society **pilgrimsfriend.org.uk**
Robopets **robopets.co.uk**
Salvation Army **salvationarmy.org.uk**

Worship aids

Patrick Coghlan, *Creating Church at Home for Older People Living with Dementia* (Kevin Mayhew, 2016).
Growing Old Gracefully **growingoldgracefully.org.uk**

Messy Vintage **messychurch.brf.org.uk/messy-vintage**
MHA Later Life Well **mha.org.uk**
Louise Morse (ed.), *Worshipping with Dementia: Meditations, scriptures and prayers for sufferers and carers* (Monarch Books, 2010).
Louise Morse and Janet Jacob, 'Brain and soul boosting: a 12 session resource to support cognition and build faith in older people', Pilgrims' Friend Society, **pilgrimsfriend.org.uk/resources/brain-soul-boosting-for-seniors**
Katie Norman and Jill Phipps, *Messy Vintage: 52 sessions to share Christ-centred fun and fellowship with the older generation* (BRF Ministries, 2021).
Siobhan O'Keeffe, *Petals of Prayer: Prayers, reflections and resources for people with dementia and their caregivers* (Kevin Mayhew, 2011).
Lindsay Pelloquin and Jaye Keightley, *Celebrating the Seasons in Residential Care Homes: A service for every week of the year* (The Paul Thomas Group, 2022).
Sue Pickering, *Creative Ideas for Ministry with the Aged: Liturgies, prayers and resources* (Canterbury Press, 2014).
Truth Be Told **truthbetold.org.uk**

Organisations and programmes engaged in older people's ministry

Anna Chaplaincy **annachaplaincy.org.uk/easy-and-church-guides**
Befriended **befriended.org**
Embracing Age **embracingage.org.uk**
Faith in Later Life **faithinlaterlife.org**
Linking Lives **linkinglives.uk**
Time to Talk Befriending **tttb.org.uk**

Notes

Introduction

1 World Health Organization, 'Dementia', fact sheet, 31 March 2025, **who.int/news-room/fact-sheets/detail/dementia.**
2 George A. Mashour et al., 'Paradoxical lucidity: a potential paradigm shift for the neurobiology and treatment of severe dementias', *Alzheimer's and Dementia* 15.8 (2019), p. 1107.
3 Tom Kitwood, *Dementia Reconsidered: The person comes first* (Open University, 1997).
4 John Swinton, *Dementia: Living in the memories of God* (SCM Press, 2017), p. 137.
5 John Killick, *Dementia Positive* (Luath Press, 2013).
6 Killick, *Dementia Positive*, p. 87.
7 Debbie Thrower, *Anna Chaplaincy Handbook* (BRF Ministries, 2022), p. 24.
8 Named after the widow Anna from Luke 2, Anna Chaplains offer spiritual chaplaincy to those of strong, little, or no faith, and promote the spiritual welfare of older people in their communities. See **annachaplaincy.org.uk** for more information.

1 Living with dementia: the journey begins

1 The several quotations by Christine herself in this and later chapters are used with her kind permission and taken from her books *Dancing with Dementia: My story of living positively with dementia* (Jessica Kingsley, 2005) and *Will I Still Be Me? Finding a continuing sense of self in the lived experience of dementia* (Jessica Kingsley, 2018), her article 'Letter to the church', *Journal of Disability and Religion*, 22.1 (2018), pp. 96–106, and an interview in *The Church Times*.

2 The several quotations by Jennifer herself in this and later chapters are used with her kind permission and taken from her book (with Louise Morse) *Dementia from the Inside: A doctor's personal story of hope* (SPCK, 2018), extracts from her website **gloriousopportunity.org**, and my personal conversations with her.

3 The several personal quotations from Robert himself in this and later chapters come from his book *My Journey into Alzheimer's Disease* (Tyndale House, 1989).

2 Living with dementia: the shared journey

1 See Michelle Cemental, '25+ inspirational quotes for caregivers', 16 May 2025, **caringseniorservice.com/blog/quotes-for-caregiver-inspiration**.

2 Steve Morris, *Memory Café: How to engage with memory loss and build community* (Grove Books, 2017).

3 Wayne A. Ewing, *In the Land of Forgetfulness: Meditations on dementia care as spiritual formation* (Wipf and Stock, 2024), p. 13.

4 The following quotes are all taken from Lucy Whitman (ed.), *Telling Tales about Dementia: Experiences of caring* (Jessica Kingsley, 2010).

5 R. Clarke in Whitman (ed.), *Telling Tales about Dementia*.

6 John Zeisel, *I'm Still Here: Creating a better life for a loved one living with Alzheimer's* (Piatkus, 2011), p. 4.

7 Henri Nouwen Society daily post, 17 October 2024.

3 Dementia and religious beliefs

1 Elizabeth MacKinlay, 'Finding meaning in ageing', *Luke's Journal* 25.3 (2020), p. 12, **lukesjournalcmdfa.com/2020/12/09/finding-meaning-in-ageing-rev-prof-elizabeth-mackinlay**.

2 Oceané Agli, Nathalie Bailly, and Claude Ferrand, 'Spirituality and religion in older adults with dementia: a systematic review', *International Psychogeriatrics* 27.5 (2015), pp. 715–25.

3 Joanna Collicutt in Robert Atwell, et al., *God in Fragments: Worshipping with those living with dementia* (Church House Publishing, 2020), p. 28.

4 'Tricia Williams, *God's Not Forgotten Me: Experiencing faith in dementia* (Cascade Books, 2022), pp. 55, 63.

5 Peter Kevern, 'What sort of a God is to be found in dementia: a survey of theological responses and an agenda for their development', *Theology* 113.873 (2010), pp. 174–82, **doi.org/10.1177/0040571X1011300303**.
6 'Tricia Williams, 'What happens to faith when Christians get dementia?', 23 October 2019, **faithinlaterlife.org/news-blog-what-happens-to-faith-when-christians-get-dementia**.
7 John Swinton, 'What the body remembers: theological reflections on dementia', *Journal of Religion, Spirituality & Aging* 26.2–3 (2014), pp. 160–72.
8 Swinton, 'What the body remembers'.

4 Faith is not just cognitive: it is a response of the whole person

1 R.T. France, *Tyndale New Testament Commentaries: Matthew* (Intervarsity Press, 1985).
2 Kenneth Lee Carder, *Ministry with the Forgotten: Dementia through a spiritual lens* (Abingdon Press, 2019).
3 Mark Wormell, *Coming to Christ in Dementia* (Mountain Street Media, 2016).
4 Carder, *Ministry with the Forgotten*.
5 John Killick, *Dementia Positive* (Luath Press, 2013).
6 From a 2020 daily email from the Henri Nouwen Society. See **henrinouwen.org**.

5 Dementia and relationships

1 BBC News, 'Dementia: wife's fear over Wellington care centre closure', 16 October 2018, **bbc.co.uk/news/uk-england-somerset-45841881**.
2 Henri Nouwen, 'Community makes God visible', 26 November 2020.
3 Kenneth Lee Carder, *Ministry with the Forgotten: Dementia through a spiritual lens* (Abingdon Press, 2019).
4 Debbie Thrower, *Anna Chaplaincy Handbook* (BRF Ministries, 2022), p. 24.
5 Gerda Saunders, *Memory's Last Breath: Field notes on my dementia* (Hachette, 2017), p. 224.

6 Nouwen, 'Community makes God visible.'
7 **memorybridge.org.**
8 Tom Kitwood, *Dementia Reconsidered: The person comes first* (Open University, 1997), p. 46.
9 Wendy Mitchell, *Somebody I Used to Know* (Bloomsbury, 2018), p. 98.
10 **symphonyoflove.net.**
11 Joanna Collicutt, *Thinking of You: A resource for the spiritual care of people with dementia* (BRF Ministries, 2017).
12 Thrower, *Anna Chaplaincy Handbook.*
13 Reneé Onque, 'Harvard happiness expert: There are 3 types of friendships—here's why you need them all', CNBC Make It, 4 September 2023, **cnbc.com/2023/09/04/harvard-happiness-expert-3-types-of-friendships-and-why-you-need-them.html.**
14 Robin Thomson, *Living with Alzheimer's: A love story* (Instant Apostle, 2022), p. 11.
15 Wayne A. Ewing, *In the Land of Forgetfulness: Meditations on dementia care as spiritual formation* (Wipf and Stock, 2024).

6 Dementia and the arts, creation, and creativity

1 Wendy Mitchell, *Somebody I Used to Know* (Bloomsbury, 2018), p. 150.
2 Christine Bryden, *Will I Still Be Me? Finding a continuing sense of self in the lived experience of dementia* (Jessica Kingsley, 2018), p. 55.
3 Houston, cited in John Killick, *Dementia Positive* (Luath Press, 2013), p. 105.
4 John Zeisel, *I'm Still Here: Creating a better life for a loved one living with Alzheimer's* (Piatkus, 2011), p. 72.
5 Makoto Fujimura, *Art and Faith: A theology of making* (Yale University Press, 2020), p. 12.
6 Oliver Sacks, cited in Killick, *Dementia Positive*, p. 106.
7 Rebecca Atkinson and Ming-Hung Hsu, 'Music has a profound affect on people with dementia', ScienceAlert, 16 October 2024, **sciencealert.com/music-has-a-profound-effect-on-people-with-dementia.**
8 Carey Smith Henderson, cited in Killick, *Dementia Positive*, p. 105.
9 See **alzheimers.org.uk/get-support/dementia-support-services/your-local-services/singing-for-the-brain.**

10 Mark Wormell, *Coming to Christ in Dementia* (Mountain Street Media, 2016).
11 Louise Morse, *Dementia: Pathways to hope* (Monarch Books, 2015).
12 Barb Noon, from the 2004 calendar 'Creativity in dementia care', published by Hawker Publications.
13 Anne-Marie Botek, 'The power of poems written by dementia patients', **agingcare.com/articles/finding-poetry-in-dementia-157152.htm**.
14 Living Words call them pieces, not poems, and say that the Listen Out Loud process is an ethical seven-step process, which does not adjust or mix a persons' words around – it strips away and does not rearrange, and is all about the validation the person feels when the words are read back with them. See **livingwords.org.uk**
15 Botek, 'The power of poems written by dementia patients'.
16 'King or Queen', *The Things Between Us* (Living Words Arts, 2014).
17 John Killick and Claire Craig, *Creativity and Communication in Persons with Dementia: A practical guide* (Jessica Kingsley, 2012), p. 45.
18 Killick, *Dementia Positive*, p. 83.
19 Zeisel, *I'm Still Here*, p. 103.
20 Messy Vintage is a gentle, sociable, and enjoyable way into worship for people in later life. It is Christ-centred, based on creativity, hospitality, and celebration. See **messychurch.org.uk/messy-vintage**.
21 Dorothy L. Sayers, *Mind of the Maker* (HarperCollins, 1968), p. 22.
22 'Tricia Williams, *God's Not Forgotten Me: Experiencing faith in dementia* (Cascade Books, 2022).
23 Robert Davis, *My Journey into Alzheimer's Disease* (Tyndale House, 1989), p. 116.

7 Living with dementia and still communicating with God

1 John Dunlop, *Finding Grace in the Face of Dementia* (Crossway, 2017), p. 11.
2 'Tricia Williams, 'What happens to faith when Christians get dementia?', 23 October 2019, **faithinlaterlife.org/news-blog-what-happens-to-faith-when-christians-get-dementia**.
3 Diane Bentley, *Lost in Time: God's grace in the midst of dementia* (Trilogy Christian Publishers, 2020).

8 'God knows me, therefore I am'

1 John Swinton, *Dementia: Living in the memories of God* (SCM Press, 2017), p. 184.
2 Elizabeth MacKinlay (ed.), *Ageing, Disability and Spirituality: Addressing the challenge of disability in later life* (Jessica Kingsley, 2008), p. 31.
3 Swinton, *Dementia*, p. 201.
4 MacKinlay (ed.), *Ageing, Disability and Spirituality*.
5 Joanna Collicutt, *Thinking of You: A resource for the spiritual care of people with dementia* (BRF Ministries, 2017).
6 John Dunlop, *Finding Grace in the Face of Dementia* (Crossway, 2017).
7 Kenneth Lee Carder, *Ministry with the Forgotten: Dementia through a spiritual lens* (Abingdon Press, 2019).
8 Mark Wormell, *Coming to Christ in Dementia* (Mountain Street Media, 2016).
9 Cynthia Fischer, 'Even dementia is not dark to God', The Gospel Coalition, 9 May 2021, **thegospelcoalition.org/article/even-dementia-not-dark.**
10 Henri Nouwen, *The Road to Peace: Writings on peace and justice* (Orbis Books, 1998).
11 Makoto Fujimura, *Art and Faith: A theology of making* (Yale University Press, 2020), p. 50.
12 John Swinton, *Raging with Compassion: Pastoral responses to the problem of evil* (SCM Press, 2018), p. 225.
13 Davidson, cited in John Killick, *Dementia Positive* (Luath Press, 2013), p. 48.

9 Learning about the needs

1 See **dementiastatistics.org/about-dementia/prevalence-and-incidence**; AgeUK, 'Living with dementia', Policy Position Paper, March 2020, **ageuk.org.uk/our-impact/policy-research/policy-positions**; Laurence Thraves, 'Alzheimer's Society's view on people with dementia living alone', Alzheimer's Society blogpost, October 2014, **alzheimers.org.uk/sites/default/files/2019-07/as_new_living_with_dementia_living_alone_update_v1_online.pdf.**

2 **lichfield.anglican.org/transforming-communities/dementia-friendly-church/dementia-friendly-church.php**
3 **pilgrimsfriend.org.uk; faithinlaterlife.org.**

10 Is this the job of the church?

1 Rupen Das, *Compassion and the Mission of God: Revealing the invisible kingdom* (Langham Global Library, 2016), p. 112.
2 **carersuk.org/policy-and-research/key-facts-and-figures.**

11 What families living with dementia want

1 **nice.org.uk/guidance/ng97/chapter/recommendations** (recommendation 1.4.2); **cogsclub.org.uk**

12 The support churches offer

1 **lichfield.anglican.org/transforming-communities/dementia-friendly-church/dementia-friendly-church.php; alzheimers.org.uk/get-involved/dementia-friends/dementia-friendly-resources**

13 Ministry beyond church attendance

1 **dementiauk.org/information-and-support/specialist-diagnosis-and-support/considering-a-care-home-for-a-person-with-dementia**
2 Oliver James, *Contented Dementia: 24-hour wraparound care for lifelong well-being* (Vermillion, 2009).
3 **growingoldgracefully.org.uk; shaftesburygroup.org; mha.org.uk; spiritualeldercare.com.**
4 **truthbetold.org.uk; messychurch.brf.org.uk/latest/projects/messy-vintage**; Lindsay Pelloquin and Jaye Keightley, *Celebrating the Seasons in Residential Care Homes: A service for every week of the year* (The Paul Thomas Group, 2022); **thegiftofyearsrugby.com.**
5 **embracingage.org.uk.**
6 **thememoryboxfoundation.co.uk.**

7 A twiddlemuff is a knitted or crocheted hand muff with various objects like ribbons, buttons, and beads attached to the inside and outside, designed to provide sensory stimulation.
8 **gloriousopportunity.org/resources/Visiting_Someone_With_Dementia.pdf.**
9 **annachaplaincy.org.uk/easy-and-church-guides**; Julia-Burton Jones, Catriona Foster, Sally Rees and Debbie Thrower, *Enabling Spiritual Care: A guide for care home staff* (BRF Ministries, 2026).

14 What's stopping us?

1 Wendy Mitchell, *Somebody I Used to Know* (Bloomsbury, 2018), p. 86.
2 Anna Dixon and James Newcome, 'Care and support reimagined: A national care covenant for England', The Archbishops' Commission on Reimagining Care, January 2023, p. 19, **churchofengland.org/about/archbishops-commissions/reimagining-care/final-report-reimagining-care-commission.**
3 Tom Kitwood, *Dementia Reconsidered: The person comes first* (Open University, 1997).
4 Graham Stokes, *And Still the Music Plays: Stories of people with dementia* (Hawker Publications, 2008).
5 **annachaplaincy.org.uk/about-the-spiritual-care-series.**
6 **caraway.uk.com.**

15 How churches could better support families living with dementia

1 Tom Kitwood, *Dementia Reconsidered: The person comes first* (Open University, 1997), p. 8.
2 Peter Kevern, 'Sharing the mind of Christ: preliminary thoughts on dementia and the cross', *New Blackfriars* 91.1034 (2009), pp. 6–7, **doi.org/10.1111/j.1741-2005.2009.01317.x.**
3 John Swinton, *Becoming Friends of Time: Disability, timefullness, and gentle discipleship* (Baylor University Press, 2016).
4 Deborah B. Creamer, *Disability and Christian Theology: Embodied limits and constructive possibilities* (Oxford University Press, 2009), p. 93.
5 James Saunders, *Dementia: Pastoral theology and pastoral care* (Grove Books, 2006), p. 15.

6 **caraway.uk.com/dementia-support/course-for-carers; embracingage.org.uk/supporting-carers-course.html.**

7 **alzheimers.org.uk/get-support; ageuk.org.uk/information-advice.**

8 **salvationist.org.uk/resources/discipleship/closer-look-dementia; methodist.org.uk/safeguarding/dementia-friendly-churches; pilgrimsfriend.org.uk/resources; faithinlaterlife.org/resources**

9 Christine Bryden, *Dancing with Dementia: My story of living positively with dementia* (Jessica Kingsley, 2005).

10 Wendy Mitchell, *What I Wish People Knew about Dementia: From someone who knows* (Bloomsbury, 2022).

11 **shaftesburygroup.org.**

12 Loren C. Eiseley, 'The Star Thrower' in *The Unexpected Universe* (Harcourt, Brace and World, 1969).

13 **menssheds.org.uk.**

Offering spiritual care in later life

About Anna Chaplaincy

Our network of Anna Chaplains offers spiritual care in later life, in a wide range of contexts. Named after the widow Anna in Luke's gospel, Anna Chaplains accompany older people in reflecting on their life and their relationship with God, breaking down generational barriers and offering prayerful presence and community.

Former broadcaster Debbie Thrower founded Anna Chaplaincy in Alton in 2010 and Anna Chaplaincy has been part of BRF Ministries since 2014. It is now led by Debbie Ducille. The network of Anna Chaplains is growing rapidly across the UK and the ministry is increasingly recognised as modelling compassionate, person-centred spiritual care for older people, as well as offering excellent training for aspiring Anna Chaplains, churches and communities.

Anna Chaplaincy is a sensitive pastoral ministry and the trademark name and logo can only be used with permission from BRF Ministries. If your church is interested in exploring Anna Chaplaincy annd Anna Friends (who support the chaplains) please email **annachaplaincy@brf.org.uk** to arrange to talk to a member of the national team.

What Anna Chaplaincy offers

Network

The Anna Chaplaincy network numbers over 430 Anna Chaplains across the UK and is growing rapidly. Anna Chaplains value belonging to the network and the opportunities it provides for support, sharing experience, learning and building community.

Training and events

Anna Chaplaincy offers a range of training events and conferences, as well as an annual network gathering. An online, six-week training course is offered several times a year, and there are regular network get-togethers, regional gatherings and themed workshops. We also run regular introductory sessions to learn about becoming an Anna Chaplain. Find out more at **annachaplaincy.org.uk/training-and-support**

Website

annachaplaincy.org.uk is a valuable resource in its own right, detailing all that the ministry has to offer. A regular blog keeps readers abreast of current developments in spiritual care for older people and helps build a strong sense of community within the network.

Resources

Anna Chaplaincy offers a range of resources, including the acclaimed *Anna Chaplaincy Handbook*, the Church Guides and Easy Guides series, and *Grief Conversations*. Our downloadable worship material includes resources to support those involved with or living with dementia.

The Spiritual Care Series

The Spiritual Care Series is a highly regarded, tried-and-tested, award-winning training course to help churches seeking to develop their ministry to older people. Find out more at **annachaplaincy.org.uk/spiritual-care-series**